MANAGING WORKPLACE STRESS

Susan Cartwright
Cary L. Cooper

SAGE Publications
International Educational and Professional Publisher
Thousand Oaks   London   New Delhi

For information, address to:

SAGE Publications, Inc.
2455 Teller Road
Thousand Oaks, California 91320
E-mail: order@sagepub.com

SAGE Publications Ltd.
6 Bonhill Street
London EC2A 4PU
United Kingdom

SAGE Publications India Pvt. Ltd.
M-32 Market
Greater Kailash I
New Delhi 110 048 India

Printed in the United States of America

Library of Congress Cataloging-in-Publication Data

Cartwright, Susan, 1951-
    Managing workplace stress/Susan Cartwright and Cary L. Cooper.
        p. cm.
    Includes bibliographical references and index.
    ISBN 0-7619-0192-2 (acid-free paper).—ISBN 0-7619-0193-0
    (pbk.: acid-free paper)
        1. Job stress. 2. Stress management. I. Cary L. Cooper.
    II. Title.
    HF5548.85.C656 1997   96-25274
    158.7—dc20

                99 00 01 02 03 10 9 8 7 6 5 4

Acquiring Editor:	Marquita Flemming
Editorial Assistant:	Frances Borghi
Production Editor:	Sherrise M. Purdum
Typesetter/Designer:	Marion S. Warren
Indexer:	Cristina Haley
Cover Designer:	Lesa Valdez
Print Buyer:	Anna Chin

Contents

1. THE GROWING EPIDEMIC OF STRESS   1

   The Next Millenium   1

   Defining Stress   3

   The Biological Mechanisms of Stress   6

   Stress and Heart Disease   8

   Stress Costs   10

   The Major Stresses of Work   13

   Plan of the Book   22

2. COPING WITH ORGANIZATIONAL
   CULTURES AND CHANGE   25

   Coping With the Psychological Culture of the
      Organization   25

   Coping With Mergers and Acquisitions   31

Adjusting to New Working Arrangements and
Career Structures   47

3. **COPING WITH THE CONSEQUENCES OF ORGANIZATIONAL CHANGE**   **52**

Coping With Job Loss   53

Coping With Middle Age: Facing Milestones   64

4. **DEALING WITH STRESSFUL SITUATIONS INVOLVING PEOPLE AT WORK**   **67**

Dealing With Difficult People   68

Dealing With Sexual Harassment   80

Coping With Unethical Behavior in the
Workplace   91

Improving Communication Within the Work
Environment   95

5. **MANAGING EVERYDAY STRESSFUL EVENTS**   **102**

Travel Stress   103

Managing Time   108

Managing Interruptions   115

Managing Workload: Working to Live or Living
to Work   119

Managing Meetings   128

Making Presentations   134

6. **HOME AND WORK**   **143**

The Changing Nature of the Family   143

Dealing With Dual-Career Relationships   146

References   **161**

Author Index   **167**

Subject Index   **171**

About the Authors   **185**

THE GROWING
EPIDEMIC OF STRESS

THE NEXT MILLENNIUM

During the 1980s, we had "The Enterprise Culture," which helped to transform economies in Western Europe and North America, as well as British industry at home and abroad. But as we were to discover by the end of the decade, there was a substantial personal cost for many individual employees, both managers and shop floor workers. This cost was captured by a single word, *stress*. Indeed, stress has found as firm a place in our modern lexicon as *fast foods*, *junk bonds*, and *software packages*. We toss the term about casually to describe a wide range of "aches and pains" resulting from our hectic pace of work and domestic life. "I really feel stressed," someone says to describe a vague yet often acute sense of disquiet. "She's under a lot of stress," we say when trying to understand a colleague's irritability or forgetfulness. "It's a high-stress job," someone says, awarding an odd sort of prestige to his or her occupation. But to those whose ability to cope with day-to-day matters is at crisis point, the concept

1

of stress is no longer a casual one; for them, stress can be translated into a four-letter word—*pain* (see Cooper, Cooper, & Eaker, 1988).

Excessive pressure in the workplace was costly to business in the 1980s. For example, the collective cost of stress to U.S. organizations for absenteeism, reduced productivity, compensation claims, health insurance, and direct medical expenses has been estimated at approximately $150 billion per year (Karasek & Theorell, 1990). In the United Kingdom, stress-related absences were 10 times more costly than all other industrial relations disputes put together. In terms of sickness, absence, and premature death or retirement due to alcoholism, stress costs the U.K. economy a staggering £2 billion per annum. Heart disease in industry, the single biggest killer, is estimated by the British Heart Foundation to cost an average U.K. company of 10,000 employees 73,000 lost working days each year; additional costs include the annual death of 42 employees between 35 and 64 years of age and lost value in products or services of more than £2.5 million. Of all absence for sickness in the United Kingdom, 21% was due to stress-related heart disease. Similarly, in Norway, the economic costs of work-related sickness and accidents amount to more than 10% of the gross national product (GNP) (Lunde-Jensen, 1994), a high proportion of which is considered stress related.

For the next millennium, it is likely to get worse. Stress is primarily caused by the fundamentals of change, lack of control, and high workload. The buildup and aftermath of the recession, the development of the European Union/North American Free Trade Association (EU/NAFTA), increasing cross-national mergers, increasing international competition, and joint ventures between organizations across national boundaries will lead inevitably to a variety of corporate "re's": reorganizations, relocations of personnel, redesign of jobs, and reallocations of roles and responsibilities. *Change* will be the byword of the next millennium, with its accompanying job insecurities, corporate culture clashes, and significantly different styles of managerial leadership—in other words, massive organizational change and inevitable stress. In addition, change will bring with it an increased workload as companies try to create "lean fighting machines" to compete in the European, Far East, and other international economic arenas. This will mean fewer people performing more work, putting enormous pressure on them.

Finally, as we move away from our own internal markets and enter larger economic systems (i.e., the EU/NAFTA, etc.), individual organizations will have less control over business life. Rules and regulations will begin to be imposed in terms of labor laws; health and safety at work; methods of production, distribution, and remuneration; and so on—all laudable issues of concern in their own right but, nevertheless, workplace constraints that will inhibit individual control and autonomy. Without being too gloomy, it is safe to say that we have in the next millennium all the ingredients of corporate stress: an ever-increasing workload with a decreasing workforce in a climate of rapid change and with control over the means of production increasingly being taken over by free-trade institutions and their bureaucracies, whether the EU/NAFTA or some larger unit in the longer term. It appears, therefore, that stress is here to stay and is not just a bygone remnant of the entrepreneurial 1980s. The purpose of this book is to highlight those aspects of people's working lives likely to be problematic in the future and what individuals might do to overcome them. Although a great deal has been written in recent years about the sources of stress, less attention has been focused on what people can do about them. In this book, an attempt will be made to redress this balance, while at the same time highlighting stressful work situations that we can begin to *de-stress*.

In this introductory chapter, we attempt to define what stress is, offer what research over the past decade has shown to be its primary sources, and provide recent examples of the costs of stress to organizations. This will help to lay the foundation for the rest of the book, which will highlight the everyday stressors likely to affect managers and employees of organizations of the 1990s and beyond and the strategies that might be used to deal with those stressors.

DEFINING STRESS

Stress is derived from the Latin word *stringere,* meaning to draw tight, and was used in the 17th century to describe hardships or affliction. During the late 18th century, stress denoted "force, pressure, strain or strong effort," referring primarily to an individual or to an individual's organs or mental powers (Hinkle, 1973).

Early definitions of strain and load used in physics and engineering eventually came to influence one concept of how stress affects individuals. Under the meaning of this concept, external forces (load) are

seen as exerting pressure on an individual, producing strain. Propo-
nents of this view claim that we can measure the stress to which an
individual is subjected in the same way we can measure physical
strain on a machine or bridge or any physical object.

Although this first concept looked at stress as an outside stimulus,
a second concept defines stress as a person's response to a disturbance.
In 1910, Sir William Osler explored the idea of stress and strain causing
disease when he saw a relationship between angina pectoris and a
hectic pace of life. The idea that environmental forces could actually
cause disease rather than just short-term ill effects, and that people
have a natural tendency to resist such forces, was seen in the work of
Walter B. Cannon in the 1930s (see Hinkle, 1973). Cannon studied the
effects of stress on animals and people and, in particular, studied the
"fight-or-flight" reaction. Because of this reaction, people and animals
will choose to stay and fight or attempt to escape when confronted by
extreme danger. Cannon observed that when his subjects experienced
situations of cold, lack of oxygen, or excitement, he could detect
physiological changes such as emergency adrenaline secretions. He
described these individuals as being "under stress."

One of the first scientific attempts to explain the process of stress-
related illness was made by Hans Selye in 1946, who described three
stages an individual experiences in stressful situations:

1. *Alarm reaction*, in which an initial phase of lowered resistance is
    followed by countershock, during which the individual's defense
    mechanisms become active.

2. *Resistance*, the stage of maximum adaptation and, ideally, successful
    return to equilibrium for the individual. If, however, the stress con-
    tinues or the defense mechanism does not work, one will move on
    to a third stage.

3. *Exhaustion*, when adaptive mechanisms collapse.

Critics of Selye's work say it ignores both the psychological impact
of stress on an individual and the individual's ability to recognize
stress and act in various ways to change his or her situation.

Newer and more comprehensive theories of stress emphasize the
interaction between a person and his or her environment. Stress was
described by researchers in the 1950s as a "response to internal or
external processes which reach those threshold levels that strain its

physical and psychological integrative capacities to, or beyond, their limit" (Basowitz, Persky, Karchin, & Grinker, 1955).

In the 1970s, Lazarus (1976) suggested that an individual's stress reaction "depends on how the person interprets or appraises (consciously or unconsciously) the significance of a harmful, threatening or challenging event." Lazarus's work disagrees with that of others who see stress simply as environmental pressure. Instead, "the intensity of the stress experience is determined significantly by how well a person feels he or she can cope with an identified threat. If a person is unsure of his/her coping abilities, they are likely to feel helpless and overwhelmed."

Similarly, Cox (1978) rejected the idea of looking at stress as simply either environmental pressures or as physiological responses. He and his fellow researchers suggested that stress can best be understood as "part of a complex and dynamic system of transaction between the person and his [or her] environment." Cox further criticized the mechanical model of stress: "Men and their organizations are not machines. . . . Stress has to be perceived or recognized by man. A machine, however, does not have to recognize the load or stress placed upon it."

By looking at stress as resulting from a misfit between an individual and his or her particular environment, we can begin to understand why one person seems to flourish in a certain setting, whereas another suffers. Cummings and Cooper (1979) have designed a way of understanding the stress process that can be simply explained:

- Individuals, for the most part, try to keep their thoughts, emotions, and relationships with the world in a "steady state."
- Each factor of a person's emotional and physical state has a "range of stability," in which that person feels comfortable. On the other hand, when forces disrupt one of these factors beyond the range of stability, the individual must act or cope to restore a feeling of comfort.
- An individual's behavior aimed at maintaining a steady state makes up his or her "adjustment process" or coping strategies.

Included in the preceding description of the stress process are the ideas described next.

A stress is any force that puts a psychological or physical function beyond its range of stability, producing a strain within the individual. Knowledge that a stress is likely to occur constitutes a threat to the individual. A threat can cause a strain because of what it signifies to the person (Cummings & Cooper, 1979).

As can be seen, the idea of stress and its effects on people has evolved from different research perspectives. Figure 1.1 summarizes these different approaches into a general overview of the concept of stress.

THE BIOLOGICAL MECHANISMS OF STRESS

Stress is clearly part of the human condition. Because of its universal occurrence, stress is not looked at in terms of its presence or absence but, rather, according to its intensity and the effect it has on individuals. Many of us seem to cope well with the pressures of work and family life that we encounter daily. But when and why is stress harmful to us? Consider what happens to the human body when it is subjected to a strain or pressure of some kind.

As Melhuish (1978), a physician specializing in stress-related illnesses, has suggested, stress is the product of many thousands of years of evolution, and human survival in a hostile environment required a quick physical response to dangers. In other words, the body "developed the ability to rev-up" for a short time. This mobilization of forces is the well-known fight-or-flight reaction mentioned earlier. "Primitive man expended this burst of energy and strength in physical activity, such as a life and death struggle with a predator."

Modern humans have retained their hormonal and chemical defense mechanisms through the millennia. But for the most part, today's lifestyles do not permit physical reaction to the stress agents we face. Attacking the boss, hitting the biology teacher who has refused to accept overdue homework, or smashing an empty automatic teller machine are not solutions allowed by today's society. Today, even the nonaggressive "flight" reaction would hardly be judged appropriate in most situations. The student who walks out in the middle of a difficult exam, the teacher who flees from a rowdy class, or the assembly worker who dashes out in the middle of a shift will likely suffer adverse consequences for their actions. Our long-evolved defense mechanisms prepare us for dramatic and rapid action but find little outlet otherwise. The body's strong chemical and hormonal

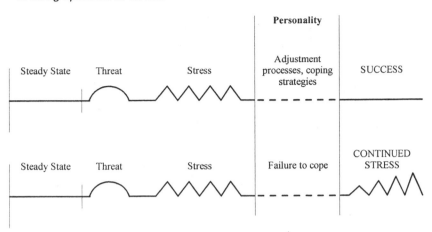

Figure 1.1. The Cooper-Cummings Framework

responses, then, are like frustrated politicians: all dressed up with nowhere to go.

This waste of our natural response to stress may harm us. Although scientists do not fully understand this process, many believe that our thought patterns regarding ourselves and the situations we are in trigger events within the two branches of our autonomic nervous system, the *sympathetic* and the *parasympathetic*. To paraphrase Albrecht (1979), in a situation of challenge, tension, or pressure, the sympathetic nervous system comes into play and activates a virtual orchestra of hormone secretions. Through this activation, the hypothalamus, recognizing a danger, triggers the pituitary gland. The pituitary releases hormones, causing the adrenal glands to intensify their secretion of adrenaline into the bloodstream. Adrenaline, along with corticosteroid hormones released through the same process, enhances one's arousal level. All these stress chemicals stimulate the brain, nerves, heart, and muscles to action.

These physiological changes combine to improve individual performance: Blood supply to the brain is increased, initially improving judgment and decision-making ability; the heart speeds up, increasing blood supply to the muscles; lung function improves; and glucose and fats are released into the bloodstream to provide additional energy. As part of these physiochemical changes, blood pressure rises (due to increased cardiac output), and blood is redeployed to voluntary muscles from the stomach and intestines as well as from the skin, resulting in the cold hands and feet often associated with a nervous disposition (Albrecht, 1979).

Although these changes result from actions of the sympathetic nerves, parasympathetic nerves can induce an opposing state of relaxation and tranquillity. As Albrecht notes, "People who have spent much of their time in an over-anxious or tense state have difficulty in bringing into action the parasympathetic branch" and its helpful capabilities.

All of the body's "rev-up" activity is designed to improve performance. But if the stress that launches this activity continues unabated, researchers believe the human body will weaken from the bombardment of overstimulation and stress-related chemicals. Many long-term effects of pressure are described by Melhuish (1978) in Table 1.1.

STRESS AND HEART DISEASE

Stress is also seen to play a part in diseases related to lifestyle, where the degree to which a person eats, smokes, drinks alcohol, and exercises plays a role. High blood pressure (hypertension) and heart disease are accepted now as having a proven link to stress. Hypertension has in most cases no obvious organic basis—it simply sets in. A majority of patients are diagnosed with "essential hypertension," meaning that the condition does not arise from any medically detectable abnormality.

Although other factors, such as diet, obesity, and smoking, surely play a role, many researchers now believe that stress is the primary cause of hypertension. The connection, as Melhuish (1978) indicates, is that hypertension is believed to result partially from changes in the resistance of blood vessels. The diameter of the arterial vessels, which carry blood to the tissues, is partly controlled by the sympathetic nervous system and its release of chemicals through the vessels. Continual activation of the sympathetic nervous system's chemical response is believed to result in reduced elasticity of the arteries and raised blood pressure. This resulting hypertension can lead to heart disease because of the increased workload on the heart as it pushes

TABLE 1.1 Effects of Stress on Bodily Functions

	Normal (relaxed)	Under Pressure	Acute Pressure	Chronic Pressure (stress)
Brain	Blood supply normal	Blood supply up	Thinks more clearly	Headaches and migraines, tremors and nervous tics
Mood	Happy	Serious	Increased concentration	Anxiety, loss of sense of humor
Saliva	Normal	Reduced	Reduced	Dry mouth, lump in throat
Muscles	Blood supply normal	Blood supply up	Improved performance	Muscular tension and pain
Heart	Normal heart rate and blood pressure	Increased heart rate and blood pressure	Improved performance	Hypertension and chest pain
Lungs	Normal respiration	Increase respiration rate	Improved performance	Coughs and asthma
Stomach	Normal blood supply and acid secretion	Reduced blood supply Increased acid secretion	Reduced blood supply reduces digestion	Ulcers due to heartburn and indigestion
Bowels	Normal	Reduced blood supply Increased bowel activity	Reduced blood supply reduces digestion	Abdominal pain and diarrhea
Bladder	Normal	Frequent urination	Frequent urination due to increased nervous stimulation	Frequent urination, prostatic symptoms
Sexual organs	(M) Normal (F) Normal periods, etc.	(M) Impotence (decreased blood supply) (F) Irregular periods	Decreased blood supply	(M) Impotence (F) Menstrual disorders
Skin	Healthy	Decreased blood supply, dry skin	Decreased blood supply	Dryness and rashes
Biochemistry	Normal: oxygen consumed, glucose and fats liberated	Oxygen consumption up, glucose and fat consumption up	Decreased blood supply	Dryness and rashes

SOURCE: A. Melhuish: *Executive Health* (London: Business Books), 1978.

blood out against a high arterial back pressure. Also, high blood pressure increases the likelihood of a possibly fatal ruptured artery; the rupture of a vessel in the brain can cause stroke. Chronic stress, and its resulting release of fats into the blood stream during the fight-or-flight response, is also believed to increase the risk of coronary heart disease by fatty deposition in the lining of coronary arteries, which carry oxygen to the heart muscle. Carruthers (1976) highlights the combination of factors that can result in a life-threatening crisis (see Figure 1.2).

STRESS COSTS

The cost of stress for a nation and for particular organizations is currently extremely high. For example, if we explore costs to the U.K. economy, the British Heart Foundation Coronary Prevention Group has calculated that 180,000 people die each year from coronary heart disease, almost 500 people a day, and heart disease accounts each year for 70 million lost working days to industry and commerce. In addition, MIND, the mental health charity, estimates that between 30% to 40% of all sickness absence from work is attributable to mental and emotional disturbance, with another 40 million working days lost to the nation's economy. The country has also suffered increased rates of suicide, particularly among younger workers, rising 30% from the late 1970s to the early 1990s. Instability and life stress have led to divorce rates rising from 27,000 in 1961 to 155,000 by 1988; they are still rising. Indeed, RELATE, the U.K. marriage guidance organization, estimates that by the year 2000 there will be 4 divorces in every 10 marriages. Finally, Alcohol Concern suggests that alcohol misuse costs society more than £2 billion per annum, with an annual cost to industry from this cause alone of nearly £1 billion. The latter group estimates that 1 in 4 men in the United Kingdom drink more than the medically recommended units per week and that between 8 and 14 million days are lost each year from alcohol-related problems, with 25% of accidents at work involving intoxicated workers. To assess your own stress levels, you may find it useful to complete the following questionaire (see Table 1.2).

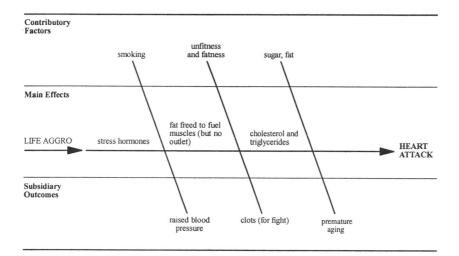

Figure 1.2. Flight Path to a Heart Attack
SOURCE: Adapted from Malcolm Carruthers, Maudsley Hospital.
NOTE: LIFE AGGRO refers to life "aggravation": stress agents at work, in the home, and elsewhere.

Who Pays the Costs?

Let's start at the beginning. Why is it that some countries (e.g., the United States or Finland) seem to be showing declines in their levels of stress-related illnesses, such as heart disease and alcoholism, while the levels of these illnesses are still rising in other countries? Is it that American employers, for example, are becoming more altruistic and caring for their employees, less concerned about the bottom line? Unfortunately, the answer is "No." Two trends in the United States are forcing American firms to take action. First, industry there is facing an enormous and ever-spiraling bill for employee health care costs. Individual insurance costs rose by 50% over the past two decades, but employers' contribution rose by over 140%. Estimates are that more than $700 million a year is spent by American employers to replace the 200,000 men aged 45 to 65 who die or are incapacitated by coronary artery disease alone. Management officials at Xerox Corporation estimated the cost of losing just one executive to stress-related illness at $600,000. In Europe, however, employers can create intolerable levels

TABLE 1.2 Behavioral and Physical Symptoms of Stress

To assess your own level of stress symptoms, indicate how often you have been troubled by the following behavioral and physical symptoms.

0 = Never or rarely
1 = Occasionally
2 = Frequently
3 = Always or nearly always

Behavioral symptoms of stress

Constant irritability with people	0	1	2	3
Difficulty in making decisions	0	1	2	3
Loss of sense of humor	0	1	2	3
Suppressed anger	0	1	2	3
Difficulty concentrating	0	1	2	3
Inability to finish one task before rushing into another	0	1	2	3
Feeling the target of other people's animosity	0	1	2	3
Feeling unable to cope	0	1	2	3
Wanting to cry at the smallest problem	0	1	2	3
Lack of interest in doing things after returning home from work	0	1	2	3
Waking up in the morning and feeling tired after an early night	0	1	2	3
Constant tiredness	0	1	2	3

Physical symptoms of stress

Lack of appetite	0	1	2	3
Craving for food when under pressure	0	1	2	3
Frequent indigestion or heartburn	0	1	2	3
Constipation or diarrhea	0	1	2	3
Insomnia	0	1	2	3
Tendency to sweat for no good reason	0	1	2	3
Nervous twitches, nail biting, etc.	0	1	2	3
Headaches	0	1	2	3
Cramps and muscle spasms	0	1	2	3
Nausea	0	1	2	3
Breathlessness without exertion	0	1	2	3
Fainting spells	0	1	2	3
Impotency or frigidity	0	1	2	3
Eczema	0	1	2	3

NOTE: Scoring: It is not the total score in each section that is important, but the number of either behavioral or physical symptoms on which you score 2 or 3. If in either category you are showing more than 3 symptoms with scores of 2 or 3, then it is indicative potentially of some current stress-related problem.

of stress for their employees, and it is the taxpayer who picks up the bill through the various national health systems. There is no direct accountability or incentive for firms to maintain the health of their employees. Of course, the indirect costs are enormous, but rarely does a firm actually attempt to estimate this cost; absenteeism, labor turnover, and even low productivity are treated as intrinsic parts of running a business (Dale & Cooper, 1992).

There is another source of growing costs. More and more employees, in American companies at least, are litigating against their employers through worker compensation regulations and laws concerning job-related stress, or what is being lately termed *cumulative stress disorder*. For example, in California, the number of stress-related compensation claims for psychiatric injury now total over 3,000 a year, since the California Supreme Court upheld its first stress disability case in the early 1970s. The California labor code now states specifically that worker compensation is allowable for disability or illness caused by "repetitive mentally or physically traumatic activities extending over a period of time, the combined effect of which causes any disability or need for medical treatment." California may be first in this regard, but what happens there has a habit of reaching other places after a longer or shorter time lapse (Ivancevich, Matteson, & Richards, 1985).

In Europe, however, we are just beginning to see a move toward increasing litigation by workers about their conditions of work. Several unions are supporting cases by individual workers, and the trend is certainly in the direction of future disability claims and general damages being awarded on the basis of work stress in the United Kingdom, as Earnshaw and Cooper (1996) highlight in their report on worker compensation and stress-related claims.

THE MAJOR STRESSES OF WORK

During the 1980s, much research in the field of workplace stress suggested six major sources of pressure at work (Cooper, Cooper, & Eaker, 1988). Although we can find each of these six implicated in an individual's stress profile or, indeed, in an organization's profile, these factors vary in the degree to which they are found to be causally linked to stress in a particular job or organization (see Figure 1.3).

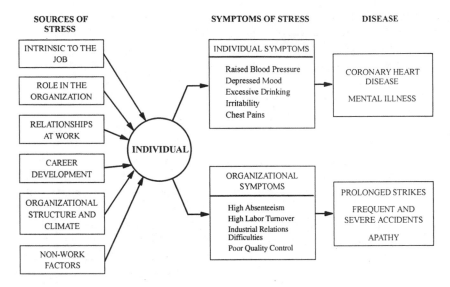

Figure 1.3. Dynamics of Work Stress

Factors Intrinsic to the Job

As a starting point to understanding work stress, researchers have studied those factors that may be intrinsic to the job itself, such as poor working conditions, shift work, long hours, travel, risk and danger, new technology, work overload, and work underload.

Working Conditions. Our physical surroundings—noise, lighting, smells, and all the stimuli that bombard our senses—can affect mood and overall mental state, whether or not we find them consciously objectionable (Cooper & Smith, 1985).

Each occupation has its own potential environmental sources of stress. For example, in jobs that require close detail work, poor lighting can create eye strain. Conversely, extremely bright lighting or glare can present problems for money market dealers.

The design or physical setting of the workplace may be another source of stress. If an office is poorly designed, with relevant personnel spread throughout a building, poor communication networking can arise, resulting in role ambiguity and poor functional relationships. This problem is not restricted to offices. For example, one company had high turnover and absenteeism among its assembly line workers, most of whom were female. When researchers looked into the problem, they discovered that the women were isolated from each other due to the layout of conveyor belts used in their work. They felt bored and lonely working without human interaction. Once the assembly line was reorganized to put them into groups, absenteeism dropped substantially.

Shift Work. Many workers today have jobs requiring them to work in shifts, some of which go around the clock. Studies have found that shift work is a common occupational stressor that affects blood temperature, metabolic rate, blood sugar levels, mental efficiency, and work motivation; shift work also influences sleep patterns and family and social life. In one study of air traffic controllers (Cobb & Rose, 1973), shift work was isolated as a major problem, although other major job stressors were also present. These workers had four times the prevalence of hypertension, and also more mild diabetes and peptic ulcers, than did a control group of second-class airmen.

Long Hours. The long working hours required by many jobs appear to take a toll on employee health. Studies have established a link between extended shifts and deaths due to coronary heart disease. In one investigation of light-industry workers in the United States, Breslow and Buell (1960) found that individuals under 45 years of age who worked more than 48 hours a week had twice the risk of death of coronary heart disease as did similar individuals working a maximum of 40 hours a week. Another study (Russek & Zohman, 1958) of 100 young coronary patients revealed that 25% of them had been working at two jobs, and an additional 40% worked for more than 60 hours a week. Many individuals, such as executives working long hours and medical residents who might have no sleep for 36 hours or more, may experience health problems and lowered efficiency at work. It is now commonly recognized that working beyond 40 to 50 hours a week results in time spent that is increasingly unproductive. Indeed, the European Community's Social Charter has specifically attempted to limit community countries to a 48-hour working week.

Travel. Although travel opportunities are appealing to many senior managers, travel itself can also be a source of stress: Traffic jams on the roads or at airports, delayed flights or trains, people, and the logistics of unknown places can present stressful challenges. Marriages and families can suffer if one member spends significant time away. In addition, a traveling manager spends less time with fellow workers and may miss out on opportunities or feel out of step with "office politics."

New Technology. The introduction of new technology into the work environment has required management and workers alike to continually adapt to new equipment, systems, and ways of working. Having a boss trained in the "old ways" may be an extra burden for the new employee trained in the latest methods, raising questions about the adequacy of supervision and employee doubts about those in senior positions.

In a study investigating sources of stress among executives in 10 countries (Cooper, 1984), Japanese executives suffered particularly from pressure to "keep up with new technology"—that is, to maintain their technological superiority. Managers in developing countries felt pressure due to the increasing emphasis on new technology, the need to deal with an inadequately trained workforce, and the imposition of deadlines. Also, in Britain, a high percentage of executives (second only to Japan) found that keeping up with new technology was a great source of pressure at work. This is not surprising in a country that privitized in the 1980s and underwent massive technological change.

Work Overload. Two different types of work overload have been described by researchers. *Quantitative* overload refers simply to having too much work to do. *Qualitative* overload refers to work that is too difficult for an individual. Quantitative overload often leads to working long hours, with the attendant problems described above. A too-heavy work burden has also been associated with increased cigarette smoking, alcohol consumption, and other stress indicators (French & Caplan, 1972).

Role in the Organization

When a person's role in an organization is clearly defined and understood and when expectations placed on the individual are also clear and nonconflicting, stress can be kept to a minimum. But researchers have clearly seen that this is not the case in many work sites. Three critical factors—role ambiguity, role conflict, and the degree of responsibility for others—are seen as major sources of stress (Ivancevich & Matteson, 1980).

Role Ambiguity. Role ambiguity arises when an individual does not have a clear picture of work objectives, coworkers' expectations, and the scope and responsibilities of his or her job. Often, this ambiguity results simply because a senior executive does not lay out for this person exactly what his or her role is. The stress indicators found to relate to role ambiguity are depressed mood, lowered self-esteem, life dissatisfaction, low motivation to work, and the intention to leave a job.

Role Conflict. Role conflict exists when an individual is torn by conflicting job demands: doing things he or she really does not want to do or things not considered to be part of the job. Managers may often feel torn between two groups of people who demand different types of behavior or who believe the job entails different functions. As might be expected, studies have shown that people with high anxiety levels suffer more from role conflicts than do people who are more flexible in their approach to life (Quick & Quick, 1984).

Responsibility. Responsibility is another organizational role stressor. In an organization, there are basically two types of responsibility: that for people and that for things—budgets, equipment, buildings, and so on. Responsibility for people has been found to be especially stressful. Studies in the 1960s revealed that responsibility for people was far more likely to lead to coronary heart disease than was responsibility for things. Being accountable for people usually requires spending more time interacting with others, attending meetings, and attempting to meet deadlines. An early investigation of 1,200 managers sent by their companies for annual medical examinations linked physical stress to age and level of responsibility (Pincherle, 1972). The older the executive and the more responsibility held by this person, the greater the probability of detecting coronary heart disease risk factors.

The stressful nature of having responsibility for others has grown in the economic climate of the 1990s, with so many industries facing cost-cutting constraints. As they implement needed cutbacks in production and sales, managers are caught between the two goals of "keeping personnel costs to a minimum," while also looking after the "welfare of subordinates" in terms of job security and stability.

Relationships at Work

Other people—in our varied encounters with them at work—can be major sources of both stress and support. This is especially so in dealings with bosses, peers, and subordinates, which can dramatically influence the way we feel at the end of the day. Hans Selye (1946) suggested that learning to live with other people is one of the most stressful aspects of life: "Good relationships between members of a group," he observed, "are a key factor in individual and organizational health." There are three critical relationships at work: those with superiors, those with subordinates, and those with colleagues or coworkers.

Relationships With Boss. Physicians and clinical psychologists support the idea that problems with emotional stability often result when the relationship between a subordinate and a boss is psychologically unhealthy for one reason or another. A U.S. study that focused on the relationship of workers to an immediate boss found that when the boss was perceived as "considerate," there was "friendship, mutual trust, respect and a certain warmth between boss and subordinate." Workers who said their bosses were low on consideration reported feeling more job pressure. Workers who were under pressure reported that their bosses did not give them criticism in a helpful way, played favorites, and "pulled rank and took advantage of them whenever they had got a chance" (Buck, 1972).

Relationships With Subordinates. The way in which a manager supervises the work of others has always been considered a critical feature of any job. For instance, "inability to delegate" has been a common criticism leveled against some managers. Managerial stress may be particularly high for those individuals with technical and scientific backgrounds, which may be more "things oriented." For these managers, personal relationships may appear more "trivial" and "time-consuming" than for managers who are more people oriented. This is particularly true of individuals promoted to management positions on the basis of their technical skills without management training; they often encounter serious relationship problems at work.

   Relationships With Colleagues. Stress among coworkers can arise from the competition and personality conflicts usually described as "office politics." Adequate social support can be critical to the health and well-being of an individual and to the atmosphere and success of an organization. Because most people spend so much time at work, relationships between coworkers can provide valuable support or, conversely, can be a significant source of stress.

   People with a particular personality—that of the abrasive, hard-driving individual—will create stress for those around them. Levinson (1973) suggests that these abrasive people cause stress for others because they ignore the interpersonal aspects of feelings and sensibilities of social interaction. Such a highly technical, achievement-oriented, hard-driving individual finds no time to cultivate amiable working relationships and so may be an important source of interpersonal stress for others.

Career Development

   A host of issues can act as potential stressors throughout one's working life. Lack of job security; fear of job loss, obsolescence, or retirement; and numerous performance appraisals—all can create pressure and strain. In addition, the frustration of having reached a career ceiling, or having been overpromoted, can induce extreme stress.

   Job Security. For many workers, career progression is of overriding importance. By promotion, people not only earn more money but gain increased status and experience new challenges. In the early years at a job, striving and ability required to deal with a rapidly changing environment are usually rewarded by monetary and promotional rewards. At middle age, however, many people find their career progress slowed or stopped. Job opportunities may become fewer, available jobs can require longer to master, old knowledge may be obsolete, and energy levels can flag while younger competition is threatening. Fear of demotion or obsolescence can be overpowering for those who believe they will suffer some erosion of status before retirement.

Job Performance. The process of being evaluated and appraised can be a stressful experience for all of us. It must be recognized that performance appraisals are anxiety provoking, for both that individual being examined and the person doing the judging and appraising. The supervisor making performance judgments faces the threat of union grievance procedures in some cases, as well as interpersonal strains and the responsibility of making decisions affecting a subordinate's livelihood.

How an evaluation is carried out can affect the degree of anxiety experienced. For example, taking a written examination can be a short-term stressor, although continuous and confidential appraisals by supervisors may exert a more long-term effect, depending on the structure and climate of the organization.

Organizational Structure and Climate

Just being part of an organization can present threats to a person's sense of freedom and autonomy. Organizational workers sometimes complain that they do not have a sense of belonging and that they lack adequate opportunities to participate; they may feel that their behavior is unduly restricted and that they are not included in office communications and consultations.

As early as the 1940s, researchers began reporting that workers who were allowed more participation in decision making produced more and had higher job satisfaction (Coch & French, 1948). Later researchers found that nonparticipation at work was a significant predictor of strain and job-related stress. It was seen to be related to overall poor health, escapist drinking, depression, low self-esteem, absenteeism, and plans to leave work (Margolis, Kroes, & Quinn, 1974). Participation in the decision-making process by workers may help increase feelings of investment in the company's success, create a sense of belonging, and improve communication channels within the organization. The resulting control, or sense of control, that participation provides seems vital for the well-being of all employees (Sauter, Hurrell, & Cooper, 1989).

Home: Work Pressures

Another danger of current economic stringencies is the effect that work pressures—fear of job loss, thwarted ambition, work overload, and so on—have on the families of employees. For instance, in the very best of times, young managers face the inevitable conflict between organizational and family demands during the early development of their careers. But during a crisis of the sort we are currently experiencing, problems increase in geometrical proportion as individuals strive to cope with basic economic and security needs. Under normal circumstances, individuals find home a refuge from the competitive and demanding environment at work, a place where they get support and comfort. But when there is a career crisis (or stress from job insecurity, as many employees now face), tensions of the job are not left behind and soon affect the family and home environment in ways that may imperil this last "sanctuary." It may be very difficult, then, for a spouse to provide the supportive domestic scene that a worker requires when the spouse is feeling insecure or is worried about the family's economic, educational, and social future.

Not only is it difficult for a housebound wife to support her breadwinning husband and at the same time cope with family demands, but increasingly, women are seeking full-time careers themselves. According to the U.S. Department of Labor, a "typical American family" with a working husband, a homemaker wife, and two children now makes up only 7% of the nation's families. In the United Kingdom, nearly 65% of all women now work, mostly full-time. Many psychologists and sociologists claim that dual-career family development is the primary culprit in the very large increase in the divorce rate over the past 10 years in the United States and countries in Western Europe.

This dual-career culture creates problems especially for women, because they are expected by men to work the "double shift," pursue a job, and manage the home (Cooper & Lewis, 1994). Women, and society at large, are discovering the myth of the New Man, who seems to exist only in the wishful thinking of women's magazine journalists! The dual-career family model also creates problems for men as well. For example, many managers and executives are expected, as part of their job, to be mobile, to be readily available for job transfers both within and between countries. Indeed, a man's promotional prospects might depend wholly on availability and willingness to accept geographic career moves. In the late 1980s and 1990s when women themselves began to pursue full-time careers, as opposed to part-time work, the prospects of professional men being available for rapid redeployment decreased substantially. In the past, these men had, with few exceptions, accepted promotional moves almost without family discussion. Now, however, such decisions will create major obstacles for both breadwinners in the family. We are already seeing this happen throughout Europe and the United States, and it is particularly exacerbated by the fact that corporations have not adapted to this changing social phenomenon. Currently, few organizations have facilities to help dual-career members of family units, particularly by career-break schemes or flexible working years.

PLAN OF THE BOOK

The stressors have been highlighted in research throughout the present and past decades. Organizations have introduced global changes to deal with some of these issues, such as improving career development, redesigning jobs, or providing counseling for interpersonal problems (Murphy, Hurrell, Sauter, & Keita, 1995). Research evidence as to the effectiveness of these interventions is encouraging, at least in the short term, and a growing number of stress reduction programs have demonstrated considerable economic savings to organizations in reduced rates of sickness and absenteeism as well as reduced health care costs (Cooper, Liukkonen, & Cartwright, 1996; Cooper & Sadri, 1991).

Most books in this field aimed at helping the individual to cope with stress have focused on health-promoting activities—for example, improved dietary habits, exercise programs, and relaxation techniques. Although their health message is important, and one we would strongly reinforce, comparatively little attention is devoted to more specific issues and situations that trouble managers and others at work and to pragmatic ways for handling them. Virtually ignored are issues such as dealing with interruptions, coping with everyday hassles in using new technology, managing the stresses of work travel, finessing bad relationships with a boss or colleague, making presentations, tolerating ineffective or debilitating meetings, and so on. These everyday hassles accumulate into *real* stress outcomes, or as

TABLE 1.3 Daily Hassles at Work Scale

Please circle the number that best reflects the degree to which the particular statement is a source of stress for you at work.

	No Stress at All		Stress		A Great Deal of Stress	
Trouble with client/customer	0	1	2	3	4	5
Having to work late	0	1	2	3	4	5
Constant people interruptions	0	1	2	3	4	5
Trouble with boss	0	1	2	3	4	5
Deadlines and time pressures	0	1	2	3	4	5
Decision making	0	1	2	3	4	5
Dealing with the bureaucracy at work	0	1	2	3	4	5
Technological breakdowns (e.g., computer)	0	1	2	3	4	5
Trouble with work colleagues	0	1	2	3	4	5
Tasks associated with job not stimulating	0	1	2	3	4	5
Too much responsibility	0	1	2	3	4	5
Too many jobs to do at once	0	1	2	3	4	5
Telephone interruptions	0	1	2	3	4	5
Traveling to and from work	0	1	2	3	4	5
Traveling associated with job	0	1	2	3	4	5
Making mistakes	0	1	2	3	4	5
Conflict with organization goals	0	1	2	3	4	5
Job interfering with home/family life	0	1	2	3	4	5
Can't cope with "in" box	0	1	2	3	4	5
Can't say "no" when I should work	0	1	2	3	4	5
Not enough stimulating things to do	0	1	2	3	4	5
Too many meetings	0	1	2	3	4	5
Don't know where career going	0	1	2	3	4	5
Worried about job security	0	1	2	3	4	5
Spouse or partner not supportive about work	0	1	2	3	4	5
Family life adversely affecting work	0	1	2	3	4	5
Having to tell subordinates unpleasant things (e.g., firing)	0	1	2	3	4	5

Americans put it, "cumulative stress disorder." Completion of the scale in Table 1.3 may help you to identify aspects of your daily work life which cause you the most stress.

The rest of this book will highlight these everyday hassles, present some typical workplace scenarios, and suggest possible ways of and techniques for dealing with them. Many of the hassles discussed emanate from fairly predictable everyday workplace occurrences; others concern more unexpected incidents, such as job loss, corporate takeover, or sexual harassment.

COPING WITH ORGANIZATIONAL CULTURES AND CHANGE

Organizational culture has an important impact, not only on how people think and behave but also on how the organization and its members are affected by and respond to changes in the internal and external environment. In this chapter, we focus on potential stressors that relate to culture and change.

COPING WITH THE PSYCHOLOGICAL CULTURE OF THE ORGANIZATION

Organizations, in functioning like minisocieties, have distinct and identifiable cultures. Organizational culture is determined by a variety of factors, including

25

- history and ownership,
- size,
- technology employed and nature of business,
- external environment and product market in which the organization operates, and
- its people, particularly founders and leaders.

Characteristically, organizational culture concerns symbols, values, ideologies, and assumptions that operate, often in an unconscious way, to guide and fashion individual and business behavior. In popular terms, it has been defined simply as "the way in which things get done within the organization." Organizational culture, like societal culture more generally, functions to create cohesiveness and maintain order and regularity in the lives of its members.

Different organizations within the same industry have different types of organizational culture. For example, the Grill Room at The Savoy and the local branch of McDonalds are both in the restaurant business, yet the experience of either working or eating at these establishments is qualitatively very different. An organization's culture is reflected in many ways and influences not only its structure and managerial style but also the way in which an organization conducts its business in the widest sense. This includes the market strategy it adopts, the type and quality of customer service it offers, and the particular kind of psychological working environment it creates for its employees.

When one joins a new organization, one must learn its culture so as to "fit into" the new work environment. This includes learning the following:

- The ways in which people interact (e.g., appropriate terms of address, the organizational jargon, acceptable forms of behavior and dress)
- The norms that govern how work is organized and conducted (e.g., reporting arrangements, preference for written or verbal forms of communication)
- The organization's self-image and the dominant values it espouses (e.g., the importance it places on particular organizational functions, the extent to which it wishes to be recognized as being "tough" or "caring" or "environmentally friendly")
- What an organization expects of employees and how it responds to customers

- How the organizational game is played and the rules for "getting along" in the organization (e.g., what it considers to be a "good" employee or an "effective" manager)

According to American psychologist Roger Harrison (1972, 1987), there are four main types of organizational culture: power, role, task/achievement, and person/support. In this section, we outline these four types and explain how to recognize them, in an effort to help employees understand how best to deal with them.

Power Cultures

The centralization of power is the most important feature of this type of culture. Characteristically, power rests with a single individual, usually the founder, or with a small nucleus of key individuals. Power cultures are generally typical of small organizations because they are often impossible to sustain as the organization grows larger, necessitating the diffusion of power; otherwise, key individuals leave. Therefore, although more frequently encountered in small entrepreneurial organizations or traditional family businesses, certain large organizations that continue to maintain a highly identifiable and often charismatic leader have managed to successfully retain a power culture. Because the emphasis is on individual rather than on devolved group decision making, power cultures have the advantage of being able to move and react swiftly, should they choose. Decisions tend to be based as much on intuition and past successes as on logical reasoning.

Long-established power cultures tend to be overlain with traditional offices, and reception areas tend to display mementos and pictures commemorating past achievements and former leaders. Because these cultures tend to retain a distinctly formal managerial style, outsiders frequently experience long-standing power cultures as being "old-fashioned" or conservative. The quality of service offered by power cultures is often tiered to reflect the status and prestige of the individual customer.

Power cultures can be further differentiated, in terms of the type and perceived legitimacy of the power exercised, into the patriarchal as opposed to the purely autocratic.

Implications for the Individual. Although in power cultures individuals are frequently motivated by fear of punishment, it is also important to recognize that in this type of culture, especially patriarchal power cultures, employee loyalty and long service are likely to be highly valued. Typically, rewards are given to the "compliant" rather than the "challenging" worker. Getting to the top frequently means maintaining visibility and ingratiating oneself with others in positions of power. It is important, if one is ever to get to know what is going on in the organization, to identify and cultivate a key informant within the power hierarchy.

To instigate any change, it is important not to "debunk the past." The best chance of getting a suggestion accepted in a power culture is to present it as a natural and logical progression that builds on what has gone before. Because power cultures are highly sensitive to criticism, it is preferable to present suggestions in a way that conveys respect for the past and, ideally, makes those in power feel as if it were their own idea. If you think that you have been unfairly dealt with or have a worthwhile contribution to make, you may have to be prepared to go over the head of your immediate boss and refer the matter to higher authority; the closer you get to the top, the more chance you have of gaining a hearing. Power cultures may be difficult to change, but once they have made a decision to change they respond quickly, so any new ideas are unlikely to get bogged down in red tape or committees. However, the best way to achieve change is undoubtedly to climb the greasy pole to the top and then change the entire culture—provided you have the stamina and willpower to do so.

Role Cultures

A role culture epitomizes the Weberian concept of bureaucracy, its guiding principles being logic, rationality, and the achievement of maximum efficiency. The organization's view of itself is as a collection of roles to be undertaken rather than a collection of people and personalities. This culture is frequently encountered in large organizations with highly specialized divisions of labor. Because commercial organizations with role cultures tend to be exclusively results oriented, finance and accounting are often recognized as being the most important functions.

In a role culture, things get done according to the "corporate bible"—usually in triplicate. Consequently, formal procedures, role requirements, authority boundaries, and regulations concerning the way in which work is to be conducted are central features of this type of culture. Power tends to be hierarchical and comes with a job description. Role cultures tend to be extremely status conscious and often breed competition between departments or divisions, particularly when budgets are discussed. One gets to know how important executives are in this organization by the size of their expense accounts, amount of budgetary discretion they exercise, type of car they drive, and quality of the furnishings of their offices. Organizations that depend on mass volume sales and standardized product quality, such as McDonalds, reflect the scripted type of customer service associated with role cultures.

Implications for the Individual. Role cultures function well in stable conditions, but their high degree of formalization, numerous committees, and so forth, make them slow to change. In the past, therefore, they offered an individual high degrees of security and a clear, sequential career path. However, although they offer predictable and reasonably fair work environments, they are frequently experienced as impersonal and often frustrating.

In role cultures, it is important to recognize that a good employee is one who recognizes protocol and sticks to the rules. One's competency will be judged above all else by an ability to fill in the "right" forms, to get the "right" signatures, and to submit them before a prescribed cutoff date. Provided that employees recognize bureaucratic priorities, master the systems, and quote the rules, nothing too dreadful will happen to them. Expertly learning ways around the systems will earn one the respect of bosses and colleagues. Employees who suggest ways in which new ideas can be incorporated within the existing system will be well received. Because role cultures nurture meetings the way horticulturists nurture plants, the ability to manage meetings and make effective presentations is extremely important for both getting along and introducing change into role cultures.

Task/Achievement Cultures

The salient features of a task culture have to do with the emphasis placed on accomplishing a given task and the energy directed toward securing necessary task-related resources and skills. Task cultures tend to exist *within* organizations (e.g., in specific departments, such as research and development) rather than as discrete organizations, although the culture is often found in new start-up organizations, particularly in new technology. A task culture is a team culture, in that commitment to the specific task bonds and energizes the individuals. The specificity of task requirements dictates how work is organized, not individuals or formal rules and regulations—*what* is achieved is more important than *how* it is achieved. Consequently, relevant expertise is highly valued and often more important than personal power or power of position.

Task cultures are characterized by their flexibility and lack of formal authority. They seek to offer their customers tailored products to meet individual needs.

Implications for the Individual. Task cultures tend to encourage creativity and autonomy and are often highly satisfying cultures in which to work. However, they do make high demands on individuals and can be exhausting and turbulent environments. To survive in such a culture, it is important to handle conflict effectively and to be prepared to give and take criticism constructively, for when things go wrong, everyone tends to blame everyone else. "Burn out" is an inherent consequence of task cultures; therefore, individuals working in this type of culture must recognize the dangers and strive to maintain equitable balances between work and leisure.

Person/Support Cultures

This culture is typified by egalitarianism. In person/support cultures, structure is minimal; the culture exists and functions solely to nurture the personal growth and development of individual members. Information, influence, and decision making are shared collectively. The organization is subordinate to the individual for its existence. Not surprisingly, in its purest form, it is more often found operating in communities or cooperatives (e.g., the kibbutz) rather than in profit-making enterprises. It may also be encountered in certain professional partnerships (e.g., of doctors, dentists, or lawyers) where there is a common agreement to share expenses for office space, secretarial services, and the like.

Implications for the Individual. Despite the emphasis on collectivism, person/support cultures can be rather isolating environments because of the emphasis placed on leaving individuals "to do their own thing." Employees within person/support cultures are encouraged to take responsibility for their own self-development, making such cultures the types of environments in which independent and highly self-motivated individuals are likely to do well.

Once individuals have recognized and learned an organization's culture, they may adapt to working *with* rather than *against* the grain of that culture and so avoid unnecessary distress. However, those who find themselves in an organizational culture in which there is a total mismatch between organizational values and their own values and preferred style of working may experience long-term stress (see Chapter 5).

COPING WITH MERGERS AND ACQUISITIONS

In the past 10 years, merger and acquisition activity has continued at unprecedented levels, both in Europe and North America. Resulting change is highly stressful to employees, because it can lead to job loss, job insecurity, and so on. In the 1980s, more than 7,000 stock-listed companies were acquired within the United Kingdom alone. At the same time, many others became party to joint venture agreements and other forms of strategic alliance, which resulted in substantially changed terms of ownership. Many of these mergers and joint ventures occurred in traditional industries, such as brewing, engineering, and manufacturing, as well as in the service sector, which has experienced considerable market consolidation in the same period. This trend toward partnering for competitiveness has increasingly involved foreign investment in U.K. companies (e.g., the Fijutsu takeover of ICL, the GEC-Alsthom engineering merger). The last decade also saw many state-owned industries become privatized, a trend that seems certain to continue. Such events, in that they have resulted in major organizational restructuring and changes in working practices and procedures, have had a major impact on the day-to-day working lives of thousands of employees.

Merger and acquisition activity may be increasing in frequency, but for workers affected, it is still an extraordinary and destabilizing life event, generating enormous uncertainty and requiring considerable personal adjustment. The magnitude of that adjustment and its associated stress has been universally rated as equivalent to the gain of a new family member or becoming bankrupt and *more stressful* than events such as mortgage foreclosure or the death of a close friend (Holmes & Rahe, 1967). Indeed, American psychologist Philip Mirvis (1985) has likened the psychological response to merger to that of personal bereavement. Another researcher, David Schweiger (Schweiger, Ivancevich, & Power, 1987), has related the emotionality in this event to the sense of detachment a young child experiences if separated from its mother.

According to Mirvis, one can expect that employee reactions to merger will pass through the four stages commonly associated with personal loss:

Stage 1   *Disbelief and Denial*
           Typically, the individual's first reaction is extreme shock. He or she may deny that the acquisition or merger will ever happen, despite circulating rumors or a bid announcement. Even when the deal is actually signed, individuals may strive to convince themselves that nothing will change. Frequently, an existing organizational leader is identified as a champion of the "status quo," one who will successfully fight to preserve the established identity and culture of the organization and not abandon, compromise, or "sell out" the company.

Stage 2   *Anger Through Rage and Resentment*
           As the reality of the situation becomes more obvious, feelings of shock and disbelief are replaced by anger and resentment toward those considered responsible. This anger may be directed toward the old management, the new merger partner, the state of the economy, the government, or even the world in general.

Stage 3   *Emotional Bargaining, Beginning in Anger and*
           Ending in Depression
           As fear and uncertainty about individual job future develops, this anger often turns inward. People become angry with themselves for not anticipating the event. They may come to resent the commitment and loyalty they previously had invested in the company. Often, they become increasingly nostalgic for what is past. Feelings of anger may subsequently subside to be replaced by depression.

Stage 4   *Acceptance*
            Finally, workers recognize that what is past is gone forever and
            accept the new situation.

Until there is acceptance that any attempt to deny or resist the situation is futile and unproductive, a positive approach will not begin to develop. Fixation at Stages 1, 2, or 3 will result in preoccupation, unproductive behavior, and negative feelings and is likely to be felt as stressful. Such rigidity may cause one to become withdrawn or perhaps leave the organization. Similarly, even if people come to accept the situation, they may still feel "let down" by their old company and no longer be as committed to or satisfied with their work or the organization. As well as dealing with the sense of loss and discontinuity at its "passing," the employees also invariably have to cope with that uncertainty associated with major organizational change and concomitant stress.

The psychological impact of merger and acquisition on individuals and its implications for personal and organizational outcomes was the subject of a large-scale research study we recently conducted (Cartwright & Cooper, 1992). This study examined experiences over time of a number of mergers, acquisitions, and joint ventures between organizations involved in the same area of business activity that resulted in wide-scale integration of two previously separate and discrete workforces. They ranged in size from small ventures, with fewer than 100 employees, to a large U.K. and pan-European merger involving several thousand employees. During the course of our study, interview and questionnaire data were collected from more than 750 individuals affected by their respective company's actions. This research is still continuing, and the database has now increased to more than 1,000 employees. Measures were taken to assess levels of organizational commitment, job satisfaction, and mental health at various points in time during the merger-acquisition process.

The model of occupational stress, presented in Chapter 1, conceptualizes potential sources of stress in the workplace as emanating from six general areas of work-related behavior and experience. Any major organizational change, such as a merger or acquisition, is likely to affect all these areas, possibly simultaneously. Therefore, it is no surprise that we found mergers and acquisitions particularly stressful because they are perceived as being an important event in an employee's working life over which one has no control. The event precipitates change that an individual has not self-selected and is psychologically unprepared for. The number and range of potential merger stressors is extensive. Although not intended to be an exhaustive list, the following are the most common stressors:

- Loss of identity, increased organizational size
- Lack of information, poor or inconsistent communication
- Fear of job loss or demotion
- Possibility of job transfer and relocation
- Loss of or reduced power, status, and prestige
- Disturbed or uncertain career path
- Changes in rules, regulations, and procedural and reporting arrangements
- Changes in colleagues, bosses, and subordinates
- Ambiguous reporting systems, roles, and procedures
- Redundancy and devaluation of old skills and expertise
- Personality and culture clashes
- Increased workload

According to Professor Jack Ivancevich (Ivancevich, Schweiger, & Power, 1987), at the announcement of a merger or acquisition, individual workers make a cognitive appraisal of the situation to determine the extent to which the event is likely to personally affect them. This appraisal may take any of the following forms:

Perceptions of the Individual of the Merger Situation	Resultant Outcome
As having no effect on the individual	An irrelevant appraisal
As a challenging opportunity for the individual	A positive appraisal
As having harmed or damaged the individual in some way (e.g., reduced his/her self-esteem or conferred a sense of powerlessness)	A negative appraisal
As potentially threatening to the individual	A negative appraisal

Because organizational communication during a merger or acquisition is often poor and there is also a considerable time lag between bid announcement and the introduction of any actual changes, individuals respond to their perceptions according to the *likely* changes that may result. Almost universally, these perceptions are pessimistic; collective uncertainty manifests itself in a wide-scale "fear-the-worst" syndrome. Consequently, negative appraisals tend to dominate.

Although the prospect of being taken over as opposed to merging might seem potentially more traumatic, our research (Cartwright & Cooper, 1992) found that, in reality, the reverse was true. Mergers create greater and more prolonged uncertainty. We found them to be more stressful and have a longer-term adverse effect on mental health than acquisitions. In support of this view, we provide evidence based on a survey of more than 150 senior and middle managers involved in a large U.K. merger in the financial services sector. Despite the lack of hostility and the high degree of cultural compatibility between the merger partners, mental health measures taken approximately 6 months postmerger integration showed more than one third of the managers surveyed with mental health scores comparable to or higher than scores of psychoneurotic outpatients. Moreover, our findings indicated that the merger had been significantly more stressful for managers of the numerically smaller merger partner.

Mergers differ from acquisitions in a variety of ways that would seem to make them inherently more stressful for those involved. Compared with acquisitions, mergers result in the following: (a) Substantially more role duplicity or overlap is likely to promote competition and jealousy as organizational members "jockey" for positions. (b) The power and resultant culture dynamics of the combination are more ambiguous. Considerable uncertainty and speculation frequently surround the issue as to "who is calling the shots." (c) Perhaps, more important, because the time between announcement and the introduction of any actual change is generally much longer with mergers than with acquisitions—a year or more is not unusual— mergers result in unacceptably long periods of "organizational limbo." Consequently, individuals feel less inclined to commit themselves to any future plans they might have had that involve major financial outlay or personal investment, such as holidays, home improvements, or further education, and they resort to "living their lives on hold."

Although the accommodation to change is often stressful, the uncertainty of anticipated change and the duration and intensity of that uncertainty have been shown to be more stressful for most people than change itself (Cartwright & Cooper, 1992). This conclusion is further supported by recent subsequent research into the effects of privatization on public utility employees (Nelson & Cooper, in press).

What Can the Individual Do?

Because of the financial importance of mergers and acquisitions, a considerable amount of managerial time and energy are expended in negotiating and completing the deal itself. Typically, such negotiations and discussions tend to center almost exclusively on financial, legal, and strategic considerations at the expense of "people" issues, which are generally forgotten or ignored.

Searby has suggested (1969) that so much energy is frequently expended at the negotiation stage, that an acquiring company's management is often too exhausted and apathetic to manage the merger effectively. Certainly, present evidence suggests the absence of any well-conceived human integration plan or management strategy for dealing with people. This, coupled with lack of sensitivity, is a common feature of most of these transactions. There are a variety of ways in which mergers and acquisitions could be managed more effectively, to alleviate or reduce stressful effects on the individuals involved:

- Provide more information and earlier involvement of the human resource function premerger, perhaps through the conduct of some form of human merger audit.
- Allow more joint consultation and opportunity for employee participation.
- Develop organizational recognition that mergers are stressful, perhaps through provision of stress management courses and counseling services.
- Provide merger telephone hotlines or appoint people specifically to confidentially and sensitively handle any postmerger grievances or anxieties.
- Create objective and fair merger reselection procedures.

Although there are many initiatives that the organization could introduce to help reduce merger distress, workers with no previous experience in this kind of situation are likely to consider their options extremely limited and so feel obliged to passively "wait and see" what happens. Prima facie, the only possible action open to them for regaining control would seem to be to seek alternative employment and physically remove themselves from a stressful situation.

There is considerable evidence that many employees do decide to take this course of action. Research studies published in the mid-1980s (Unger, 1986; Walsh, 1988) report levels of voluntary resignations among senior executives as high as 25% to 50% in the first year postmerger. Abnormally high rates of labor turnover following mergers and acquisitions are not exclusively confined to senior managers and occur at all levels of the organization. Cartwright and Cooper (1992) found that the overall rate of staff turnover across all levels of employees, even during a period of economic recession, can be in certain circumstances as high as 60%. However, resigning may not necessarily be a sensible or practical course of action, especially if motivated by anger or outrage. This is particularly the case for older or long-serving employees who may risk losing potentially substantial unemployment payments or jeopardize or disrupt established pension arrangements.

Breaking Out of the
Fear-the-Worst Syndrome

Universally, the most stressful aspects of mergers and acquisitions are fear of job loss and living with uncertainty. Fearing for survival, typically, workers are likely to be reluctant to admit to others in the workplace, particularly superiors, the degree of stress they are experiencing because this may jeopardize any job future by indicating that the worker is not "merger-fit." Consequently, most merger stress remains covert and "bottled up" during work time and is expressed or discussed only at home with relatives, close friends, or colleagues.

Of individuals surveyed postmerger by Cartwright and Cooper (1992), 78% considered that the merger had caused them some degree of stress. Twenty percent reported that they had coped badly and had not developed any effective strategy for dealing with the situation. Approximately 25% said that the main strategy used to combat stress was talking with a spouse or partner. Although the social support of family and friends is an important and useful strategy for coping with stress, because the consequences of major organizational change may have important family repercussions (e.g., job loss or relocation), endlessly speculative discussions around the dinner table of the plethora of "nightmare scenarios" of what might happen serve only to heighten anxiety at home. Talking about the situation may make the individual directly affected feel better, but doing so may effectively transfer stress to a partner.

Typical Scenario

John Jones, a 37-year-old regional sales manager, is married with a dependent wife, Ann, two young preschool children, and a large mortgage. His company announced a merger with a considerably larger operation. John feels his position is particularly vulnerable because of overlap in sales territories. This fear is shared by his sales team. Rumors are already circulating that his territory will soon come under the hammer. He is aware that his most successful sales representative has been approached by a competitor.

Because John is concerned that subpar performance by his team will affect the outcome of any "carve-up" of his territory, he is anxious to maintain morale and keep his team motivated. Consequently, at work, he tends to play down the situation and tries to convey a business-as-usual attitude and not disclose his own anxieties.

When these anxieties surface at home, Ann has always been interested in and supportive of his career, so each evening he discusses his merger-related worries with her. His wife listens sympathetically but feels totally impotent to alleviate his fears. Searching for reassurance and advice, she takes to discussing John's situation with her friends and neighbors. This serves only to increase her anxieties. Friends empathize, but it seems that each of them has a bad luck or merger horror story to tell about unfairly and insensitively displaced executives.

Ann becomes increasingly angry and irritated with John for burdening her with the anxieties of a problem she feels powerless to resolve, his obsession with the merger, and his resultant lack of interest in her life. She finds herself unable to "switch off" his situational angst and continue with her own day-to-day activities. She becomes "snappy" with her children. Moreover, she comes to dread John's return home and his endless recitation of the latest rumor or counterrumor. Before long, she becomes less sympathetic and is no longer prepared to listen to her husband's endless monologues; she acts to avoid any discussion of the matter. John becomes upset by his wife's apparent uncaring and unsupportive attitude; relationships at home deteriorate and he starts to regularly call in at the pub on the way home.

Outcome. Originally, John had problems at work; now he also has problems at home. His one strategy for dealing with the distressing situation, externalizing his worries by talking to Ann, is no longer available. Drinking may temporarily obliterate the negative mental dialogues and inner turmoil he is battling with, but it is more likely to exacerbate his problem rather than solve it. In the long term, his work performance and psychological health will likely be adversely affected and increase the likelihood that he will lose his job.

Alternative. Many problems associated with mergers and acquisitions stem from lack of official communication, lack of information, and fear of the unknown. This void in communication is then automatically filled by rumor and scaremongering. In a merger situation, rumors that travel the farthest and fastest are invariably negative. There is seldom anything more pervasive than collective misery. In drawing parallels with other merger experiences, stories of merger casualties are more likely to be remembered than those of successful merger survivors. Because rumors are verbally communicated, they are particularly vulnerable to distortion and exaggeration, as anybody who has ever played the game of "Chinese Whispers" (or "Gossip") will recognize. Attending to rumors is a mentally torturous and unproductive activity.

Rather than confront the rumors with his superior, John responded by sharing his fears exclusively with his spouse. Although there are benefits to be gained from openly discussing anxieties with others, unfortunately, John went into "overkill" and effectively destroyed any support that Ann was originally prepared to offer. Ann's support may have helped John vent his feelings and possibly put the situation into a more rational perspective, but she was not in a position to dispel the veracity of the rumors or reassure John that his job future was secure. Hence, her own increasing feelings of powerlessness.

John may think it helpful and necessary to talk things over with Ann. However, he would have found her support more likely to continue if there had been some prior negotiation and acceptance on his part of Ann's position. They might have agreed to restrict discussion of his merger problems to a mutually agreed-on and ruthlessly enforced preset time limit, perhaps setting aside a half hour each workday evening for discussion, rather than letting it dominate their entire conversation. He could have acknowledged that the purpose of these discussions was mainly to help him express his feelings and that he did not expect Ann to come up with any solutions. John and Ann could have built on their strong family relationships, rather than threaten them, by planning and becoming more involved in family activities and making the merger subject totally taboo on weekends. These choices would have allowed them to work toward a more positive and in-formed evaluation of their situation.

Avoiding Negative Mental Monologues: Seeking Alternative Constructions

As discussed, how an individual perceives any event or situation dramatically affects the stress response experienced. The announce-ment of a merger or takeover represents a crisis or critical point in an individual's working life. Certainly, it is a time to take stock and to reassess achievements to date, in both the work and personal domain. The Japanese word for *crisis* means both a threat and an opportunity. Often in such circumstances, it is the perception of threat, and fear of the worst, that makes the event so stressful. To deal with merger stress more effectively, one must reverse the usually negative mental mono-logues or self-talk that do nothing to mitigate stress and, instead, focus on more constructive and positive ways of viewing a given situation. Thought stopping, or the ability to recognize nonconstructive thoughts, attitudes, and behaviors and halt them immediately, is an extremely effective strategy for coping with stress. One influential senior executive of long standing is reported to have a sign in the hallway of his home, directly opposite the front door, that reads NOW STOP THINKING ABOUT WORK!! This sign is probably an extremely effective trigger for this man to put aside problems of the day that, in any event, he cannot solve until the morning.

In a merger situation, it is important for an employee not only to recognize and stop nonconstructive thoughts and attitudes but also to replace them with more constructive self-talk alternatives.

Typical mental monologue: Oh, God, I shall lose my job.

Alternative construction: I might not necessarily lose my job, but if it should happen is that really the worst possible outcome? I will still have things that I value more—good health, family, and friends. Was I really that happy with my job? If I were to be let go, are there alternative jobs or goals that I might pursue but that my present situation prevents me from doing?

Personal Stock Taking. It's also helpful to conduct a personal inventory, as shown in Table 2.1.

Formally conducting this kind of exercise serves several useful purposes:

- It can put the work situation into perspective.
- It can help identify or stimulate ideas of possible alternative job and career options.
- Prior analysis of personal strengths and achievements in terms of what the individual has to offer this (or any subsequent organization) can be beneficial in positively enhancing self-concept and can serve as helpful preparation for any subsequent merger reselection interview.
- It directs the individual toward nonwork-related and family goals. Work-related goals may be temporarily "on hold" at this time, but there are likely to be other nonwork-related goals that the individual could focus on and move toward during this period of uncertainty. Many of these (e.g., learning a foreign language, improving interpersonal skills, etc.) may necessitate an investment of time rather than any substantial financial commitment. As well as providing a useful diversionary activity, this would also help workers to regain a sense of control over an aspect of their lives and combat the numbness and behavioral inertia often associated with mergers. Focusing on goals that involve skills development is likely to improve psychological health and may also enhance future career prospects.
- Reviewing personal financial matters at the outset, may help pinpoint areas of unnecessary expenditure where cutbacks could be made in the future, should the worst happen.

Completing this activity at this time is likely to be valuable in helping people focus more positively on the future rather than dwelling in the past and so move the them to a state of psychological acceptance of the situation. However, life-planning reviews should not be conducted exclusively in response to a crisis but, rather, become an exercise that one undertakes on a regular basis. Many life goals are not achieved overnight and require systematic planning; otherwise, they never move beyond the realm of wishful thinking. Recent research (Holmes & Cartwright, 1993) has found that although many individuals desire to change their careers in midlife, those who successfully achieve a career change are more likely to have researched and planned specific moves a long time in advance.

TABLE 2.1 Taking Stock

	In the Work Domain	In the Personal Domain
Your personal strengths and weaknesses		
Your skills and talents		
Your achievements		
Times and occasions when you really felt good about yourself		
Past opportunities that you regret not taking		
What you have to offer the organization		
What the organization had to offer you		

	Work Related	Nonwork Related
Your short-term goals (for the next 6 months)		
Your mid-term goals (for the next 5 years)		
Your long-term goals (5 years and beyond)		
The short-, mid-, and long-term goals of other members of your family		
Your financial assets and liabilities		
Your monthly expenses (i.e., first-priority expenses)		

Typical mental monologue: Things will never be the same again; the culture will change and everything will be different. Past experience and loyalty will count for nothing. There'll be a new man at the top with new ideas who will bring in all his own people. It'll be a case of change, change, change . . . and more change and all for the worse!

Alternative construction: Sure, there will be change; it might be for the worst. But equally, things might get better. This organization is not perfect and certainly could be improved. If I give it a fair chance, once I get used to it, I might prefer working in the new merged organization. The increased organizational size, combined strengths, and stronger market position might actually improve my future job security and create more opportunities not fewer.

Organizational Stock Taking. A great deal of merger stress is created by fear of the unknown. Altendorf (1986), in his study of the Getty-Texaco combination, concluded that the first thing organizational members do in a merger or takeover situation is to make assessments and draw conclusions about "the others'" culture. For the majority of employees, assessments made prior to any actual physical or sociocultural integration are likely to be based on rumor, secondhand reporting, and implicit theories and involve inference rather than firsthand knowledge or experience. When the partnering organization is also foreign, assessment of the other culture is likely to be conflated by perceived national stereotypes. For example, in the 12 months leading up to the legal announcement of a recent U.K. merger, when questioned, many employees were unable to give consistent and accurate basic information as to the number of people employed by the partnering organization or their site locations. Furthermore, it was found that perceptions of what the other organization was like were largely based on impressions extrapolated from national brand advertising.

Gaining more factually based knowledge about the acquiring organization or other merger partner, and its culture, is one way of reducing the perceived threat and critical mass of the unknown. Such information is now always forthcoming from "official" sources within the organization; however, this does not preclude individuals from learning more for themselves. Company reports, product literature, supplier/customer research, and business directories are often more reliable sources of information than in-house rumors or local newspapers.

Research into the impact of culture change on the individual (Cartwright & Cooper, 1989, 1992) has shown that the experience is not always negative. It might depend on (a) the extent to which individuals value their own culture and (b) their perception of the degree of attractiveness of the new or other culture. In other words, the experience is likely to lead to increased job satisfaction, if valued aspects of the existing culture (i.e., rituals, practices, procedures, etc.) are accommodated and retained and are supplemented or integrated with the more desirable aspects of the culture of the combining organization.

Because from the outset, mergers and acquisitions are invariably responded to as "win-lose" situations, there is a collective tendency for individuals to fight for and resist change in every area of organizational activity for fear of conceding "ground" to the other.

In such situations, working alone or with your immediate work group, it can help to give some thought to the following questions:

> What things about your current organization (i.e., values, systems, practices, managerial style, etc.) would you not like to see changed?

> What things about your current organization would you like to see changed or may even in the past have tried to change without success?

> What are the main areas for improvement?

> What do you *actually* know about the acquiring organization or other merger partner? What would you like to know?

> What do you expect will change?

> What do you *hope* will change?

In completing this exercise, you have now identified the potential areas of change that are likely to cause you anxiety and, possibly, stress, as well as those areas where you would positively welcome change. Consequently, you are starting to move from a negative and resistant psychological state to a healthier, more positive and rational negotiation mode, which will be beneficial in responding and discussing any proposed changes in the future. The maintenance of a flexible, as opposed to a rigid, mental attitude is important in reducing the stress response.

A number of more progressive organizations, with whom we have worked in such situations, have conducted large-scale acquisition and merger surveys to ascertain employee response to questions similar to the preceding. This information has proved extremely valuable in guiding integration decisions and creating an agenda for negotiation and discussion.

Maintaining Life as Normal

Robert Frost once wrote "the reason why worry kills more people than work is that more people worry than work." Certainly, all of us at some time or another spend a considerable amount of unproductive time worrying and agonizing over events that *never actually happen*. As parents of teenage children, we worry about their possible drug involvement, yet the overwhelming majority of teenagers still reach adulthood without ever having experimented with drugs. Similarly, parental concern about juvenile crime has reached hysterical levels, yet reported crime statistics show that over the past few years, there has actually been a reduction in juvenile crime.

Awareness of the potential danger or threat of a situation is a more constructive alternative than turning a blind eye to it or than naïveté, but it is qualitatively different from worry. Worry is a consuming, often paralyzing and dysfunctional, emotion that serves no constructive purpose and results in stress.

As already discussed, to deal with merger stress more effectively and so reduce its potentially negative impact, it is important to "switch off" concerning rumors and maintain a balanced perspective. Rumors stem from collective insecurity. Often, there are so many contradictory merger rumors circulating that, rationally, they could not possibly all be true. Deliberately avoiding or limiting the time spent engaging in or listening to "rumor sessions" at work and focusing on more immediate tasks or life goals is a desirable strategy. Avoidance behavior, such as taking a walk at lunchtime or playing a game of squash rather than sitting around in the break room discussing the merger with coworkers and risking becoming more depressed, is not only useful but also has the advantage of improving physical health.

If you become aware of a persistent and worrisome rumor that directly affects your work, take steps to confront it with your superior or union representative. Ask for any *specific information* about the situation (i.e., what does he or she know?) rather than seeking subjective opinions (i.e., what does he or she think?) or asking about other rumors that might be making the rounds. He or she may allay your fears. More often than not, that person will be as much in the dark as you are. If so, it is important to accept that as the situation rather than automatically assume that he or she knows something but is not prepared to tell you, and so increase your paranoia. Managers should recognize that they have a responsibility to regularly and consistently brief subordinates on merger-related matters, even if the content of that briefing is only to reaffirm that, at the current time, there is little or no information to communicate.

Many individuals in takeover and merger situations feel that they and their jobs are "on trial" and so become obsessed with personal survival. As a result, they often act to promote a desirable image of themselves that might impress those whom they perceive as influential in the decision-making process. Typical behavioral manifestations include working longer hours, piling their desks with files, playing politics, belittling the contributions of others, and generally getting themselves noticed. The effort, pretense, and, often, social isolation of affecting or exaggerating behaviors that are uncharacteristic of the individual are likely to be stressful in themselves and have detrimental long-term psychological consequences. Furthermore, in the long term, they are likely to serve no useful purpose whatsoever in that they may be misdirected toward the "wrong" decision maker(s). Or the transparency of such behaviors will be recognized and will either be ignored or despised. It is far better to maintain a flexible and open mind, but at the same time remain true to yourself, than attempt to read (possibly misread) the situation and so be forever adjusting your behavior in what is likely to be an unstable and changing environment.

Finally, although work routines may have been disrupted, it is important to maintain one's nonwork and health routines.

ADJUSTING TO NEW WORKING ARRANGEMENTS AND CAREER STRUCTURES

In recent years, the dynamics of the labor market have changed dramatically. Advanced technological developments and the demands of an increasingly competitive marketplace have changed the business strategies, structures, and cultures of many organizations. Notably, there is now an increasing emphasis placed on performance measurement and target setting for jobholders at all levels within the service industries. Effects of these changes have been most pronounced in banking, insurance, and financial service sectors; they have radically altered employee working practices, skills, requirements, and career structures. For many employees in both public and private organizations, the resultant change toward a more sales-oriented and performance-driven culture has challenged traditional core values associated with white-collar occupations—for example, employment security and "job-for-life" concepts.

Technology in the Workplace

Since the 1970s, growth in workplace automation, particularly computer technology, has steadily increased and revolutionized traditional office environments. Between 1990 and 1995, 50,000 jobs were lost in the United Kingdom in financial, professional, and business service sectors; most of the job loss was the result of new technology. Typically, this was the consequence of computerized banking, the introduction of automated share transfer systems in the major financial institutions, and the gradual dismantling and rationalization of branch networks to provide more cost-efficient service to the retail customers through establishment of regionalized teleservicing centers. Besides affecting job security, the introduction of advanced technology requires employees to develop new competencies. Such technology is also often perceived as a means for deskilling (or dumbing down) jobs and reducing personal freedom and privacy. For some workers, an estimated quarter to one half of all knowledge-based workers by the year 2000, it may even mean that home becomes the workplace. Current estimates suggest that between 5%

and 15% of all U.K. companies employ at least a few home-based teleworkers.

On one hand, technology opens up opportunities for more flexible working arrangements, enabling people to work away from a centralized workplace. But it may also make work more socially isolating, reducing social interaction and physically restricting workplace movement. Often, technology also affects physical working conditions, by increasing heat and noise levels in the environment. It may deprive workers of the psychological need and satisfaction of physically handling things (such as documents, files, etc.) and the associated tangible sense of achievement.

Research on the impact of technology in the workplace has found mixed evidence as to whether computers increase job interest and perceived skill use. However, a number of studies suggest that computers are thought to increase workload and time pressure. Liff (1990) conducted a study of more than 200 female clerical workers in the West Midlands who had experienced technological change. Forty-five percent reported an increase in workload. Almost 40% reported that office automation had resulted in increased stress. Another study, of video display unit (VDU) operators in the insurance industry (Bradley, 1983), found that compared with nonusers, computer users felt more hurried and stressed, were more subject to frustration at work, and considered their work pace as too fast.

A major source of frustration for computer users is system response time and breakdown. From evidence adduced by Johannson and Aronsson (1984), there appears to be a generalized tendency among VDU operators to pace themselves at a higher rate in the mornings to guard against breakdowns. Actual breakdowns, and also the expectancy of breakdown, can become an appreciable mental strain, especially for those who deal directly with customer inquiries.

Inadequate training and lack of consultation in system design and introduction appear to be common sources of frustration and stress reported by computer users. Overall, Liff (1990) concludes that although technology may change the nature of the job itself and increase task variety for some, it can also reinforce the current gender division of labor in the office and reduce career advancement opportunities, largely for women.

Performance Measurement and Target Setting

At the same time, new structures and technology have produced heightened attention to performance and the introduction of performance-related pay schemes as well as the incorporation of new performance criteria into appraisal systems (Sparrow, 1995). Particularly within the banking, insurance, and financial service sectors, employees at all levels are now increasingly required to be more sales oriented, outgoing, and competitive and to cross-sell additional services to existing customers as an integral part of their jobs. As organizations have become more committed to providing cost-efficient customer service quickly, and in a variety of places and times, white-collar employees are now required to be more flexible and work outside traditional office hours.

Increasingly, monitoring systems have been developed to provide managers and supervisors with the type of performance indicators previously associated with manufacturing output. Systems that monitor the average number of key strokes per minute, average call-handling time, and the rate of production and error levels now exist in many organizations and serve to reinforce employee perceptions that Big Brother is watching.

The effects of monitoring practices have been the center of much debate recently (Piturro, 1989). Performance monitoring and other forms of organizational surveillance have been regarded by critics as "an invasion of privacy and ultimately denigrating to employees" (Nussbaum & du Rivage, 1986). Advocates deem these procedures "essential to conducting business and largely beneficial to employees in terms of the capability to instruct them in their work" (Chalykoff & Kochan, 1989) by providing feedback to the employee and ensuring customer satisfaction. In an important study by Di Tecco, Cwitco, Arsenault, and Andre (1992) looking at stress among telephone operators, monitoring practices were found to contribute significantly to feelings of stress. Piturro (1989), reporting on organizations presently using or having used monitoring techniques, noted that in companies such as AT&T and Federal Express, where monitoring practices were discontinued, productivity and service quality remained at high levels. Furthermore, Federal Express reported a notable increase in job satisfaction and reduction in stress and anxiety.

Stress emanating from performance measurement and monitoring would seem to be associated with lack of control, loss of trust, and an increased administrative workload involved in operating such reporting procedures. The continuing emphasis placed on closely monitored employee performance, directly linked to reward and advancement, often rests uncomfortably alongside the concept of empowerment and participative management practices, particularly if employees are not consulted in the establishment of targets or the selection of performance criteria.

The Changing Nature of Work and Career

The collective impact of recent changes in work and work organization has changed the security and rules implicit in the employment contract. This has already manifested itself as growth in outsourcing many aspects of business activity and in the trend toward short-term employment contracts. Typically, this has resulted in status differentiation within organizations between "permanent," "temporary," "core," and "peripheral" workers. These changes have also transformed the informal relational or psychological contract between employer and employee.

This psychological contract has been defined (Rousseau, 1990) as "a set of expectations held by an individual employee that specifies what the individual and the organization expect to give and receive in the working relationship." Research suggests that this contract has important implications for employee attachment and commitment to the employing organization, as well as for individual career expectations (Robinson & Morrison, 1995). Implicit in the terms of such contracts is the notion of mutual exchange and benefit to both parties. Traditionally, under the terms of the *old* contract, generated in a period of relatively high and stable employment, the majority of individuals entered organizations expecting to receive steady financial rewards, investment in training, assured opportunities for career advancement, and a relatively high certainty of job security in return for hard work, loyalty, and demonstrated commitment to the organization. In certain perceived high-risk occupations—for example, sales and marketing— lowered expectations in job security were usually offset by higher levels of financial rewards. In terms of career management, the role of employer was typically that of a nurturing parent, whereby employees exchanged compliance for security (Spindler, 1994) and trusted the organization to recognize, develop, and reward their talents and achievements with career promotion.

In contrast, under the terms of the "new" psychological contract, organizations expect employees to be more flexible, more accountable, and to be hardworking and committed; at the same time, employers offer increasingly limited (or no) assurances or expectations of employment security and career development opportunities. It is not hard to imagine that for significant numbers of future workers, the job is likely to become a freelance activity in the form of a series of temporally or discretely defined tasks or projects undertaken either successively or concurrently for single or multiple employers. For this, the individual receives financial payment, negotiated in advance, either on a fixed-cost basis or dependent on results achieved.

The impact of these new psychological contracts on organizational performance, employee commitment, and motivation will deservedly become the focus of considerable research attention in the future. However, for those individuals currently working in "delayered" organizational structures, coping with changed career expectations requires considerable personal adjustment in terms of attitudes and mind-set. To make that adjustment, one must accept that the onus for career management and training now rests with oneself rather than with the organization. This requires a greater degree of self-initiative and personal planning and control. Rather than inhibiting personal development, individuals can optimize their situation by enhancing their skills, introducing greater task variety, challenge, and stimulation in their work by using lateral opportunities to work in different departments or functions. The model of career development increasingly being presented by researchers in this field is one of a career spanning several organizations rather than a single lifetime employer (Herriot, 1995). Inherent in this model is the notion that employees should seek to develop "employability" and that workplaces should provide opportunities for that rather than providing employment. To individuals, this means availing themselves not only of training opportunities existing within the organization but also looking to external agencies, such as local colleges. Although the prospect of pursuing a self-determined career outside the structure of an established organization might seem daunting, research evidence (Holmes & Cartwright, 1993) based on experiences of midlife career changes suggests that a pursuit of increased job and life satisfaction is frequently gained from a move to freelancing and self-employment.

COPING WITH THE CONSEQUENCES OF ORGANIZATIONAL CHANGE

> *Peter Hardy, a bank manager, threw himself off the cliffs at Beachy Head, in East Sussex, after being made redundant from Barclays. Mr. Hardy, 45, of Speen, Buckinghamshire, who joined Barclays when he was 18, drove to the cliffs two days after being offered early retirement, an inquest in Eastbourne was told. Coroner's verdict: suicide.*
>
> —from the *Times*, Friday, March 12, 1993

This poignant extract illustrates a desperate response to a situation that has become increasingly more commonplace in recent years. That Peter Hardy, a relatively young man with possibly 20 or 30 years of active life still ahead of him, should choose to end his life so prematurely encapsulates the extreme misery and sense of rejection that many people experience following job loss and the importance and meaning that work gives to an individual's life.

COPING WITH JOB LOSS

Although money is a primary motive for work, for the vast majority of workers having a job is more than just having a source of income. Studies examining reasons that people go to work (Warr, 1982) have found that 69% of men and 65% of women in the U.K. workforce would continue to work even if there was no financial necessity to do so. Work serves a variety of functions for the individual:

- It imposes a time structure on the day.
- It provides an opportunity to use existing skills and acquire new ones.
- It gives one the opportunity for interpersonal contact with people outside the family.
- It creates activity and variety.
- It defines individual goals and purposes.
- It defines aspects of personal status and identity.

Consequently, when a person loses his or her job, the sense of loss experienced extends beyond the forfeiture of a regular paycheck.

Unemployment increases the individual's dependency on others, both physically and psychologically. Not only must this person come to terms with living on a reduced income—typically estimated at between 45% to 60% of one's working salary—he or she must also accept, besides the financial loss, being dependent on others (i.e., the state, family members, financial institutions, money lenders, etc.).

Characteristically, unemployment presents a range of common problems that are potential sources of distress to the individual. First is *loss of identity*. In personal and societal terms, a job generally defines who one is, where one lives, the people one mixes with, and one's status in society. Women who voluntarily leave their jobs to become full-time mothers frequently report experiencing not dissimilar problems concerning loss of job-derived identity. From the outset, giving birth is a significant social leveler. To midwives, visiting nurses, and other hospital staff members, all women who have babies are undifferentiated and responded to as "mothers"; previous career and occupational status is of little or no importance. For the career woman who decides to stay at home with her young family, this newly defined identity of mother in some way displaces and erases whatever went before. For many women, reclassification to being "*just* a housewife," to talk about what she was in terms of the work she used to do as if it were a previous incarnation, requires considerable adjustment. However, the birth of a baby does in itself confer a new role and form of work; although it may have less status and be less socially valued, motherhood nonetheless provides activity and purpose. Unfortunately, the same cannot be said for unemployment.

Because of the loss of temporal structure, activity, and purpose provided by work, unemployed people often become demotivated and have great difficulty filling their day. Consequently, as research has shown, they spend a great deal of time watching TV, sleeping, and sitting around. The limited availability of money restricts opportunities for activity and social contact outside the home and, as a result, frequently places considerable strain on family relationships.

One of the most difficult problems faced by the unemployed is coping with the *uncertainty* of the situation. When an individual becomes unemployed, there is no way of knowing how long it will be before he or she finds another job. This presents major dilemmas, especially concerning decisions to cut back on expenses—for example, "trading down" to a smaller house or moving to a less desirable suburb. Maintenance of existing lifestyle, by borrowing or using unemployment compensation payments, may ultimately prove disastrous if the work loss becomes long term. Similarly, the panic selling of assets in a falling or depressed market may be costly and result in unnecessary distress if the individual is able to gain reemployment in a relatively short period of time.

An uncertain job future can have a serious impact on *self-esteem*. Any initial optimism is likely to soon be eroded in the face of a rising pile of rejected job applications, particularly in a recessionary job market. Fears develop that existing skills will deteriorate over time if not used, and self-esteem and confidence decline. As high unemployment rates have increasingly become a feature of the U.K. economy in recent years, the social stigma attached to unemployment has become less marked than it was. However, especially among older workers and those out of work for the first time, there still remains the cultural remnants of a strong work ethic, which causes people to feel guilty or apologetic about not having a job.

Therefore, although for some, unemployment may present a blessed relief from the tedium of boring, dissatisfying, or physically debilitating work, it is for many a major life event with unprecedented negative financial, physical, and psychological consequences. As research has consistently demonstrated, although work may be stressful, having no work is even more stressful. Evidence from studies conducted by Warr (1987) and his colleagues at Sheffield University revealed that employed people are on average psychologically and physically more healthy than those who are unemployed. The impact of job loss on psychological health is typically rapid. Within 3 months, mental well-being is significantly impaired; it subsequently stabilizes, rather than continuing to decline, after a 6-month period of unemployment. Furthermore, compared with employed men, the evidence suggests that unemployed men are significantly more likely to die during the following decade; the differential probability is particularly marked for suicide and death from lung cancer (Warr, 1987).

Recent unemployment trends indicate that job loss tends to be heaviest among older workers, those who find it most difficult to find new employment (Social Trends, 1990). Approximately 60% of males aged 50 to 59 and 35% of males aged 35 to 49 remain unemployed for 2 years or more, compared with 23% of males aged 25 to 34 (Holmes & Cartwright, 1993). The chances of gaining employment are greater for female workers. At least 50% of all women under 50 remain unemployed for fewer than 26 weeks. Compared with men, women are more likely to take up part-time or lower-paying jobs.

The disproportionate burden of job losses borne by older workers may be explained by their overrepresentation in long-established, declining industries (e.g., primary industries and manufacturing) and their underrepresentation in new and expanding industries, coupled with the tendency of employers to dismiss older workers in all industries. Since 1980, U.S. manufacturing companies have dispensed with more than 2 million workers (Cascio, 1993). Corporate restructuring, or "downsizing," has been a major contributor to white-collar unemployment. According to Cascio (1993), in the period 1982 to 1991, more than 85% of the Fortune 1000 companies downsized, with a loss of more than 5 million white-collar jobs. The impact of unemployment tends to be felt most by single persons, single-income families, and especially middle-aged workers. For the latter, job loss often corresponds with other life stage crises. Unemployed middle managers in their early 40s probably still have dependent children to support, yet their chances of gaining reemployment, compared to younger workers, are perceived to be lower because they are more likely to encounter the problem of ageism and, frequently, are less geographically mobile. Similarly, compared to those over 50, they are less likely to be well cushioned financially and are too young to take early retirement.

In Chapter 2, we discussed the individual's response to merger and acquisition in the context of a four-stage bereavement model. This model is equally appropriate in understanding how individuals respond to job loss, even when they lose jobs that they did not find particularly enjoyable. Because the time spent at work consumes so much of our daily lives, for most people its loss creates as great a void as does the loss of a close family member or friend. Outplacement consultant Max Eggert (1991) relates the story of how Margaret Thatcher, on losing her premiership, felt so lost without her usual tightly packed timetable that she even became confused about what day of the week it was.

Coping With the Shock: The Early Days

Although we will focus on more practical aspects of unemployment and job search, it is important to be aware of the emotional cycle associated with the event. The initial surprise or shock of losing a job invariably causes one to "freeze up" and be unable to make any plans. A common response is to minimize or trivialize the event. Many people, after becoming unemployed, react by taking a holiday or going on a spending spree, as if to convince themselves or those around them of the insignificance of their loss. They may even procrastinate about seeking advice or unemployment benefits. From initial shock will come anger and bitterness. Much of this anger will be outwardly directed: One may resent one's former employer, or family and friends, especially if they still have well-paid or satisfying jobs. This stage often represents a high-energy period when the jobless person is prone to sudden and frequent outbursts of temper or frantically applies for any kind of job, whether or not he or she meets entry criteria. Irrationally, the individual may even expect a call from his or her former employer, contritely offering the old job back after having realized that the company was wrong to let that person go in the first place.

To better cope with this difficult period, it is important for individuals to recognize that the feelings they are experiencing are normal and, in time, can be worked through. During the early days, people who have lost their job should intuitively accept that they are likely to behave irrationally. Therefore, we suggest several appropriate responses:

- Most important, keep reminding yourself that *jobs*, not *people*, are made unnecessary. Jobs may become valueless and obsolete, but people do not. Rather than being a crisis, job loss can turn out to be an opportunity. Even Prime Minister John Major had a period of unemployment in his career.

- Do not panic and risk acting with unnecessary haste. Allow some time to calm down and get over the initial shock. A few days away and a change of scenery may help; however, it is a far better idea to plan to take a holiday *after* you have found a new job or at least have a clearer idea of your future plans.

- Inform your mortgage lender or bank that you have lost your job. As unemployment has escalated, financial institutions have developed a more sympathetic attitude toward borrowers who find themselves in this situation and are prepared to negotiate remedial financial arrangements. Foreclosure is not an imminent problem in the early days following job loss, so do not make yourself ill worrying about it!

- Do not procrastinate about "signing on" or making inquiries about available unemployment benefits. The system was intended as a safeguard to help people in this situation. You paid hard-earned contributions while working, so there is no need to feel ashamed about using a service you have helped to fund. Most people do not expect their homes to burn down and to be made homeless, yet if such an event should occur, they do not feel embarrassed about making an insurance claim. In principle, the social security system operates in a similar way as an insurance policy to protect individuals from unfortunate and unintended life accidents and hazards.

- Be open to others about your situation; they may prove helpful in providing you with contacts that could lead to a job. Contact with others in the same predicament, through a job club or similar self-help group, can also be a valuable means of social support. However, joining such a group in the very early days, when one is still extremely angry and bitter, may be counterproductive by further fueling or prolonging that anger or leading to depression.

- To begin your job search, you will need to prepare a curriculum vitae (CV). Many individuals find this difficult to do in the early days following job loss, or they may make a poor attempt. There are a number of possible reasons for this:

1. Having received a major blow to self-confidence and self-esteem, jobless persons do not feel sufficiently positive about themselves to present themselves in a way that will impress potential employers.

2. It may have been such a long time since they last had to prepare a CV that they lack the necessary skills.

3. In preparing a CV, jobless individuals are forced to make a tacit public admission that they are without work.

■ Therefore, before rushing to the typewriter to chronologically document your work history, first conduct the kind of personal stock taking outlined earlier (see Coping With Mergers and Acquisitions in Chapter 2) to assess your strengths and weaknesses. Asking friends and associates who know you well for their opinions can be helpful in this regard. Documenting previous achievements is beneficial in that it helps us recall times when we felt good about ourselves. Reliving past successes, or giving oneself "positive strokes," has enormous psychological value. It is also often useful to ask others about the kinds of jobs they think you might be good at.

■ Finally, resist the temptation to apply for each and every job advertised regardless of its suitability. When it comes to finding a job, the number of interviews or offers you are likely to receive does not increase proportionately to the number of applications made, particularly if you disregard or fail to meet the criteria specified. Rather, it will result in a disproportionate number of depressing rejections, notably if your CV is rushed and ill prepared, which will only serve to further and unnecessarily erode self-confidence.

Coping in the Longer Term

As we have already discussed in earlier sections, anger is counterproductive, and the sooner this is recognized, vented, and exhausted, the better. While jobless individuals remain fixated at this stage, they are most unlikely to make any positive and realistic career plans. Even if a person is fortunate enough to obtain a job interview, he or she is liable to communicate this anger to the interviewer, with negative results. After anger comes depression. Sometimes, before depression occurs, it is preceded by what is termed the *fantasy effect* or avoidance behavior, whereby one mentally focuses on so-called rescue scenarios. Such scenarios are either unlikely to happen (e.g., getting one's old job back, winning the lottery, etc.) or they represent situations that the individual is not prepared to act on (e.g., alternative career ideas, such as setting up one's own business). Such fantasies can be temporarily comforting and are a way of avoiding the reality of seeking work and so risking rejection. Anger, fantasy, and depression are also normal responses of the emotional cycle; however, sufferers who remain in any of these states for a prolonged time should promptly seek professional counseling.

As the number of preretirement courses now available indicates, it has become increasingly recognized that even giving up a job voluntarily requires systematic preparation and professional advice if individuals are to cope effectively with their change in lifestyle. Joblessness requires a similar approach that extends beyond a sympathetic attitude and a copy of the help-wanted section of the classified. In recognition, many, more progressive, large organizations now provide what is termed *outplacement* facilities to support and counsel those who are compelled to leave an employer to enter the next stage of their careers. Such facilities vary in terms of the standard and type of services and assistance they provide. They may be run in-house or be provided by external outplacement consultants, of which there are currently more than 120 in the United Kingdom. Such services are often quite expensive and are frequently restricted to fairly senior personnel. However, after losing you job, it is worthwhile to ask your former employer what assistance can be provided. It may be only to agree that you continue to use your company car for the next month while you sort yourself out. In this section, we suggest a variety of positive steps that will help in moving through the job loss cycle.

Preparing a Systematic Job Search Campaign

Consider All Possibilities. For individuals who have lost jobs in a declining industry, it stands to reason that they will likely experience difficulty in finding alternative jobs in that same industry. Any job opportunities that do arise will attract a large field of similarly placed candidates, and if they are successfully reemployed in that industry and it continues to decline, they face the likelihood of becoming jobless yet again in the future.

It is, therefore, important to consider a job search not just in light of the work you have been doing but also in light of what you could or would like to be doing. Typically, initial career decisions are based on incomplete information and, often, little real knowledge of what the day-to-day work involves. Early career choices are often influenced by factors such as parental or peer pressure, images portrayed by the media, high starting salaries, and attractive "perks" or glossy recruitment literature rather than by aptitude and personality. Career satisfaction is, therefore, more a matter of chance than choice. However, even if a "good" choice is made initially, over time, a career can often become inappropriate or dissatisfying as different stages in the life cycle are reached and attitudes and values change. Loss of a job can, therefore, present an opportunity for reappraisal and a chance to make a fresh and invigorating new start.

Research (Holmes & Cartwright, 1993) indicates, notably for those over 35 years of age, that the most popular career change is toward the autonomy of careers and jobs such as self-employment, lecturing, teaching, or consultancy. Between 1979 and 1989, the number of self-employed people in the United Kingdom rose by more than 70% from just under 2 million to around 3.25 million. Many individuals who move to self-employment report substantially increased job satisfaction, especially if they are able to turn a hobby into a job. Changing careers may seem like an interesting but daunting prospect, yet tens of thousands of those who leave the armed forces each year have been successfully making that transition for years.

A variety of information sources offering career advice are available other than at job centers and job clubs:

■ *Career consultants:* A number private consultancy practices offer career guidance. Usually, they are run by or employ the services of an occupational psychologist. Typically, their assessment and consultation process involves in-depth interviews and the completion of a series of psychometric tests and questionnaires to ascertain individual aptitudes and suitability for certain kinds of work or training. In addition to advice on potential career paths, many outplacement organizations also provide guidance and skill training for CV preparation, interview techniques, and so forth.

■ *Local-authority careers service:* All large towns and cities have state employment offices that can be useful sources of information on jobs, training, university courses, and the like. Many also provide specific adult guidance services. Local libraries are also potential sources of career information; many institutions of higher and further education run short courses that may be useful to the unemployed in areas of skills training, starting up a new business, and so on. Help in this area is also available in the United Kingdom from local-enterprise agencies or the Training and Enterprise Council (TEC).

■ *Self-help manuals and courses:* There are many helpful publications, such as *Build Your Own Rainbow* (Hopson & Scally, 1993) and the 1995 edition of *What Color Is Your Parachute?* (Nelson-Bolles, 1995). The Open University also produces a relatively inexpensive self-development pack composed of work books, self-assessment questionnaires, and other materials designed to help individuals realize their potential.

Constructing a Curriculum Vitae. These documents are vitally important as a marketing tool for securing a job interview. But in itself, a CV does not get people hired—people, not a CV, get jobs. The CV should include, besides standard, personal biographical information, your work experience, beginning with your most recent employment; a summary of your educational qualifications; your aptitudes; professional or trade associations to which you belong; your interests; and a statement of your achievements, both work and nonwork related. In the United States, it is illegal for employers to ask age-related questions on application forms or at interviews. If you consider that disclosing your age may result in unfair discrimination, do not include it unless specifically directed to do so.

In the past, it was the convention to prepare a CV using a strictly chronological format. In recognition that the prime objective of a CV is to capture the interest of its recipient, alternative, more distinctive and dynamic forms have been found more effective. A CV that provides a powerful up-front section that briefly summarizes experiences and achievements and gives a kind of 20- to 30-second "commercial" or postcard-sized advertisement of oneself can be especially effective. Rather than plowing through pages of historical information, the reader is immediately provided pertinent information that captures one's attention and prompts one to read on, if the candidate sounds interesting.

Again, many publications provide useful guidelines about preparing a CV. For example, *Super Job Search* (Studner, 1989) is an excellent source for professionals and managers. Consider a few basic tips:

- A CV should not be too long—no more than 3 pages.
- A CV should be typewritten or handwritten in black pen so that it can be easily photocopied by potential employers.
- Use short, punchy sentences; avoid jargon.
- Experiment with layout, headings, margins, and the like. (Software packages can be most useful in this regard.)
- Say more about your recent work experiences and less the further back in the past you go.
- Always enclose a cover letter with the CV. Putting your CV into a folder or clear plastic holder is also a good idea. This will ensure that it remains in pristine condition. Accidents happen (i.e., accidental damage, coffee spills, etc.), that may unfairly detract from its appearance.

Alternative Methods of Job Search. Apart from responding to advertised job openings, be aware that nearly 70% of managerial jobs are never so listed. Networking through informal contacts, sending out a speculative CV directly to potential employers, or using employment agencies can enhance your possibilities.

Polishing Up Interview Techniques. The art of successful interviewing or being interviewed is an extensive enough topic in itself to be the subject of an entire book. Indeed, you will find many such books in local bookstores, libraries, or private employment agencies. However, advanced preparation is of fundamental importance:

- Do some prior research about the target company: its size, product range, location, and so forth.
- Draw up a list of questions you expect to be asked, including those you would most not like to be asked (you can be fairly certain that a skilled interviewer will ask them). Plan, and then practice, your answers with others in a role-play situation. Other people can provide useful feedback on how clear, convincing, or enthusiastic your answers sound.
- Draw up a list of questions you would like to ask about the company and its products.

- Allow ample contingency time so that you do not risk arriving late for your interview. Take with you a spare copy of your CV in case it has been misplaced and also so you can refer to it during the interview.

Coping Emotionally

Many jobless individuals would probably consider a systematic job search a full-time job in itself. However, almost everyone is likely to encounter periods when "time hangs heavy." It is important to maintain the discipline of getting up reasonably early in the morning, getting dressed, and planning the day's activities. Physical appearance can often become neglected when one spends most of the time at home and has little contact with people other than immediate family or friends. By investing in an answering machine, one will not miss important job-related messages yet will not feel housebound and unable to get out in public. As research has shown, physical health often deteriorates following job loss. It is important, therefore, to continue to eat sensibly and regularly and to undertake some form of regular physical exercise. Exercise is beneficial, not only for improving physical fitness but also because the resultant improvement in body shape enhances self-image and the exercise provides an outlet for anger and aggressive feelings. Fears concerning the deterioration of existing skills, loss of purpose, and loss of social contact outside the house can often be overcome if a person continues to work in a temporary, part-time, or voluntary capacity. It is not that unusual for such activities to develop into full-time paid employment. Gaps in employment on a CV raise eyebrows; however, providing evidence of continuing work in a part-time or voluntary capacity or of having taken further training demonstrates motivation and commitment to maintain and develop existing skills. Working in volunteer jobs with people less fortunate than oneself can also be intrinsically rewarding and help a person put his or her own situation in perspective.

One out-of-work executive tells the story of how he was successful in gaining an interview, but when the interviewer realized his age he said he was really looking for a much younger man. The executive suggested his willingness to work on a stopgap basis until the organization found someone they considered more suitable. The organization agreed, and 10 months later, the executive was still working there and found himself being offered a permanent job. There has been an increasing trend toward temporary and stopgap managerial positions. A publication called *The Directory of Interim Management*[1] gives information on organizations that provide this service.

COPING WITH MIDDLE AGE:
FACING MILESTONES

Age is something that creeps up on us. Suddenly, we reach a point in our lives when we realize that "old" is no longer a label that applies only to others around us; it now also applies to us. Apart from the obvious physical signs of aging, certain life events psychologically remind us of our mortality (e.g., loss of our parents, the death of a member of our peer group, the birth of a grandchild, an invitation to join a preretirement course).

According to psychologist Donald Super (1957), there are four broad, age-related career stages. The first stage, *exploration,* typically occurs between ages 15 to 24. This is when individuals form ideas about themselves and the world of work, explore opportunities, and make choices as to the type of career and organization to which they are most suited. From the mid-20s to early 40s, they move into the second stage, *establishment.* This stage represents a period when the need to achieve and prove oneself is often very strong. During this time, people are typically concerned with directing their energies toward securing themselves in their careers and climbing "the greasy pole." It is also a time when many individuals are coping with the financial and emotional demands of raising a family and establishing themselves in society more generally. From mid-40s until retirement, the *maintenance* stage, individuals then become more concerned with hanging on and maintaining the position they have achieved rather than looking to advance further. Earlier career optimism has by now usually been curbed by realism or, possibly, pessimism. Finally, these workers enter the fourth stage, which Super terms *decline.* Decline is characterized by a decreasing involvement and participation in work and is usually reached by age 65+.

Traditionally, the idea of midlife crisis was associated with age 40. However, fueled by many youthful examples of people from the world of show business who have continued to produce popular hit records or remain "box office idols" beyond their 40th birthdays, coupled with increased life expectancy, there is now a certain widespread credibility to the slogan that "life begins at 40." This has arguably had the effect of making the next age milestone—passing 50—critically more important.

Passing age 50 is a significant change for the average male, because testosterone production begins its slow decline around this time. From puberty through middle age, the production of this hormone increases proportionately with male aggression, competitiveness, self-confidence, self-reliance, and assertiveness. Around the age of 50, glandular production of this hormone begins a gradual decline, with consequent changes in boardroom as well as bedroom behavior.

Most top managers are male, and after 50 is the time for them to enjoy life, broaden interests, and change pace. But one must take control: People who are driven have to make sure that they are doing the driving rather than the system's driving them. They have made big contributions in their careers, so now may be the time for them to get a better match for what they want and need.

The most vulnerable group are executives in their late 40s and 50s, who are also likely to be abusing alcohol and coping with alienated children, aging parents, and extensive financial commitments. But it is still the minority of these individuals who are damaged by such problems and challenges. If people manage their remaining careers correctly and review their management styles, they can cope with the challenges and maintain the excellence of their contributions, along with keeping the "buzz" in their working lives.

Taking Stock at Age 50

Where are you going to from now on? Torrington and Cooper (1990) recommend five options:

1. *Consolidation.* Settle for doing even better what you are already doing quite well. Of all the mountains you have climbed, the one you are at the top of now is where you are going to stop. Instead of looking for new things to do, find ways of doing the present things better. Let others do the pathbreaking while you concentrate on quality of product, people, and performance.

2. *Transfer.* Try a lateral move so that you apply your expertise and experience in positions that are different from what you do now but similar. This may be simply a change of colleagues, or it may

involve deploying familiar skills in a different way. This will give you novel challenges and the opportunity to work in different social settings.

3. *Diversification.* Add variety rather than load to your portfolio. Instead of continuing to do everything in your job, let other people pick up some of the opportunities while you spend more of your time on management development within the business or on charity work outside it. Your expertise is potentially valuable in all sorts of ways other than making money. Spread it around a little; cast yourself in a different role for a few hours a week. Not only will you enjoy it, and perhaps do some good, you will also learn a lot and get a better perspective on the job you have been doing all your life.

4. *Change.* Change is risk, because you take up a totally different type of work, as in becoming a schoolteacher or training for the priesthood. How is your humility? You will need plenty if you are going to move from the field in which you have been a success to start anew as a nonentity. There is always a dash of romance about this sort of bold move, which is often made by those seeking a degree of fulfillment that has hitherto escaped them. Diversification is safer, because you maintain your position and status as an expert at the same time that you are learning new ways.

5. *Step down.* Most logical, this move is actually the hardest. It is an absurd belief that top managers can only move up and never down the hierarchical pyramid. If you move down, you are stigmatized; there must be something wrong with you. Either you have failed or are ill. This is less a problem in other walks of life. In our university, leading academics take it in turn to assume roles as dean, vice principal, and head of department. They serve for 2 or 3 years and exercise considerable authority before reverting to their traditional academic roles. Lawyers, medical practitioners, and actors all expect to change status within their professions at different times of their lives. Managers must soon break with the convention that corporate careers are one-way streets, simply going up or nowhere.

NOTE

1. Available from Robert Baird, 75 Manor Way, Blackheath, London, SE3.

DEALING WITH
STRESSFUL
SITUATIONS
INVOLVING
PEOPLE AT WORK

The people we work with can be a great source of stress or, conversely, create the environment and support to make life at work worth living. Our dealings with bosses, colleagues, customers, and subordinates can dramatically affect our productivity and health and, indeed, the way we feel at the end of each day. Hans Selye (1946), the father of stress medicine, once said, "Good relationships between members of a group are a key factor in individual and organizational health." Even the prominent fiction writers of our time recognize the importance of relationships in the workplace. The main character in Joseph Heller's (1975) book, *Something Happened*, reflects on his relationships in an insurance company: "In the office in which I work there are five people of whom I am afraid. Each of these five people is afraid of four people (excluding overlaps), for a total of twenty, and each of these twenty people is afraid of six people, making a total of one hundred and twenty people who are feared by at least one person." He goes on in terms of his own department: "There are six people who are afraid of me, and one small secretary who is afraid of all of us. I have one other person working for me who is not afraid of any, not even me, and I would fire him quickly, but I'm afraid of him." Although humorously portrayed, most of these sentiments strike a psychological cord with many of us.

This chapter will explore difficult or problematic relationships at work and what can be done to cope with them. We examine relationships with the boss, colleagues, and clients and customers, as well as employee problems in general. We will start with probably the most significant and important relationship we have in the work setting—our relationship with the boss.

DEALING WITH DIFFICULT PEOPLE

Managing the Boss

We frequently read in management textbooks about the "hows" and "whys" of managing people at work, particularly subordinates or colleagues. We rarely ever hear, however, about managing a relationship with the boss—the central relationship we have in the workplace. Understanding how to manage bosses requires a special awareness of the different types of bosses, their personality needs, management styles, and sanctioning behavior, and most important of all, an awareness of those coping strategies that might be most successful in managing them. This section will highlight and explore the different species of bosses in an effort to understand how best to deal with them in an organizational context. We will draw heavily on the work of Makin, Cooper, and Cox (1988), highlighting various prototypic bosses they describe—the bureaucrat, the autocrat, the wheeler-dealer, the reluctant manager, and the open manager—what they are like, and how to cope with them. Of course, rarely will any particular boss fit just one of these types. If you want to influence your own boss, however, you've got to know him or her and be prepared to take offensive or defensive action. Remember, as George Bernard Shaw once wrote in *Mrs. Warren's Profession,*

People are always blaming their circumstances for what they are. I don't believe in circumstances. The people who get on in this world are the people who get up and look for the circumstances they want, and if they can't find them, make them.

The Bureaucrat

The bureaucrat is generally pleasant and mild mannered but is often excessively slow and cautious in making decisions. When faced with a problem or suggestion, his or her usual response is to suggest that you check to see if the idea is in accordance with established custom and practice. If the problem or the suggested solution is novel, the bureaucrat probably will advise the questioner to send memos to all those who are likely to be affected, asking for their reactions. According to Dean Acheson, former U.S. Secretary of State, the basic rule of a bureaucrat is that memos are sent not to inform the recipient but to protect the sender. Subordinates would be well-advised to read all memos when dealing with the bureaucrat.

In addition, a committee or working party might be formed to advise or decide on the issue. If you, as a subordinate, do anything in a way that is not sanctioned by the organizational rules and procedures, then you are likely to receive a reprimanding memo. This memo will be in addition to any possible verbal reprimand and will be concerned with the way you went about the task rather than with the outcome. Thus, you may actually be praised for what you accomplished but admonished for breaking the rules to get the task done. These responses tend to have a demotivating effect on subordinates, who tend not to bother taking any initiative. If you want a quiet life, you learn how to work within the rules.

Personality Needs. Not unlike most managers, a bureaucrat will probably have a great need for power. The main expression of this is this person's need to control others, which can be achieved in a number of ways. According to McClelland (1961), these range from sheer domination to subtle influencing techniques. Bureaucrats exercise control through strict administration of the rules. In this way, a high degree of certainty and predictability can be achieved. When their needs are blocked by higher authority, they tend to follow new instructions to the letter, waiting for a collapse so that they can say, "I told you so!"

Management Style and Sanctions. Bureaucrats tend to be authoritarian but will stay within the rules and their own limits of sanction. They may use powers granted by the organization when dealing with subordinates. These are generally those of *position power,* based on their position within the organization, and *resource power,* based on their control of rewards. When dealing with superiors, they will generally be compliant, but if they believe that rules are being broken, they may use their control of information as a source of power. For example, this control may be used positively, by "leaking" information damaging to a superior, or negatively, by holding back information that would allow the system to take corrective action.

How to Cope. The best approach for dealing with this type of boss is to know the rules and regulations of your organization so that you can present proposals in such a way that they are seen to be consistent with the system. If this is not possible, then avoid pushing your preferred, and possibly innovative, solution. Rather, present the problem, together with your own "tentative thoughts" on the matter, as a request for help. Under these circumstances, bureaucrats often show considerable ingenuity in redrafting your thoughts to fit the current system or finding alternative interpretations of the rules.

The Autocrat

Autocrats have very strong views on what ought to be done in any situation. These are derived from their own personal convictions concerning what should be done rather than from the organization's rules. They do not listen very well to their subordinates, and they issue instructions that they expect to be carried out without question. Such managers are intolerant of those who make mistakes and people who "do not understand." They will get quite angry in these situations but in a cold, withdrawn manner. Sometimes they appear inconsistent, because although they are autocratic with subordinates, they are often helpful to their peers and respectful in relations with someone higher up the organization. In the eyes of their subordinates, they can be either tyrants or benevolent autocrats, depending on their personal style.

Personality Needs. Both autocrat and bureaucrat express a great need for power, but the former's source of power resides in personal convictions, not in the rules of the organization. There is research evidence to suggest that those with a high need for power are sensitive to power differentials, as Cox and Cooper (1988) highlight. Autocrat's behavior may vary, however, depending on whether the difference is in their favor or not. This would explain apparent contradictions in their responses to different groups in the organization. If the balance is in their favor, as it is with subordinates, then direct power can be used. Faced with those who have greater power, they gain power by ingratiating themselves. This can be done by doing favors or flattering the more powerful individual. There is evidence to show that those managers with a high need for power do, in fact, respond positively to such ingratiation from subordinates. With their peers, the autocratic manager can gain some temporary increase in power by giving help when asked, especially if the other manager then feels in some way obligated.

Management Style and Sanctions. Like the bureaucrat, the autocrat will use those sanctions that his or her position in the organization provides. These are, as before, position power and resource power. If the organization accepts it, they may also employ *coercive power.* The benevolent autocrat is likely to use resource power quite effectively, giving infrequent, unpredictable, but large, rewards.

How to Cope. As with bureaucratic types, confrontation should be avoided unless on the basis of data. Because of the autocrat's need for power, a technique of ingratiation is often most effective. Again, because of this need, the autocrat is sensitive to power from other sources. If the subordinate has more *expert power* than the boss and is prepared to stand up to the autocrat, this may be respected. In general, if you have a source of power that is unavailable to your boss (normally, expert knowledge or information), then often, he or she will cultivate the relationship. This is, however, a high-risk strategy and should be tried with care. The information or expertise you have may be of only temporary value. Movie mogul Sam Goldwyn, by all accounts an extreme autocrat, reportedly said that he did not want to be surrounded by yes-men. He wanted subordinates to tell him the truth, even if it cost them their jobs!

In extreme cases, autocrats are often brought down by a grouping of subordinates. Realizing that their individual powers are not strong enough to confront the autocrat, political alliances are made between subordinates, so as to increase their power base. An act by the autocrat that clearly and seriously breaks the organization's rules often becomes a trigger for concerted action by the subordinates. The autocrat is either removed, or his or her powers are strictly defined and limited, often by devolving power to a committee.

The Wheeler-Dealer

Wheeler-dealers are often very senior managers who spend much of their time negotiating with other departments over allocation of resources and such matters as purchasing and sales. They clearly enjoy this type of activity and, as a result, spend a lot of time doing it, leaving their own departments very much to run themselves. They are not always successful in the negotiations, possibly because they are impatient and do not "suffer fools gladly." When in their own departments, they will make "sorties" around staff, asking how they are getting on, checking on the progress of various projects. Staff members are not given much guidance and are often left to sink or swim, but initiatives by staff are usually well supported. Nonperformers tend to be ignored. There is a general feeling of dynamism in the department but also a certain amount of chaos.

Personality Needs. The wheeler-dealer is almost certainly an innovator type, and if achieving objectives means that rules have to be ignored, so be it. We suspect that most are also high on achievement, hard-driving Type As, but there is no reason why some should not be Type B. Their need for power is probably high. Because they know other people are necessary for them to achieve their objectives, this need is more socialized than in the autocrat or bureaucrat. Control is achieved by interpersonal influence rather than by coercion.

Management Style and Sanctions. Style may range from consultative to participative to laissez-faire. They often delegate quite considerably but sometimes, especially in moments of stress, may show a flash of authoritarianism. Often, they will regret this when things cool down and later try to smooth ruffled feathers. They frequently use personal power, and people will work hard for them because of the admiration they inspire. Approval is withdrawn from subordinates not performing up to the mark.

How to Cope. With this boss, it is essential to become proactive. Wheeler-dealers expect staff members to use their own initiative, and they value only those who do. It is no use waiting to be told what to do—nothing will happen and you will be written off as ineffective. You should be prepared to make your own decisions about what needs to be done and then get on with the task, making sure that the boss is kept informed. This boss should be informed rather than asked, the assumption being that you will go ahead unless there are objections. Keeping the boss informed also means that you maintain a high profile with him or her. Problems with this type of boss often center on getting the more mundane jobs done. The boss does not get pleasure from boring tasks and, likewise, does not reward those who do them, no matter how well. As a result, people learn that doing mundane jobs does not pay off. Often, these jobs are thrust on the most junior staff members (*junior* in terms of seniority or tenure). If you're in this position, you should negotiate with colleagues to ensure that boring tasks are shared evenly. Depending on your colleagues, it may be possible to do this by open agreement, or it may be a more political process. Because the boss values enthusiasm and energy, find something to be enthusiastic about and hook his or her excitement; then point out that mundane jobs are preventing you from devoting your energies to it.

The Reluctant Manager

This person will have been promoted on the grounds of technical competence. Reluctant managers generally let their departments run themselves, and they do not encourage staff in any way. At the extreme, they could be described as "people who go around stirring up apathy." If a technical problem arises, they will offer help if asked, and this help will be highly effective. The management of the department, both internally and externally, is ignored. In some circumstances, however, the reluctant manager may appear to be bureaucratic. Because he or she is not interested in managing, following the organization's rules provides the easy way out. When something nonroutine happens, it is often very difficult to get a decision of any sort from them.

Personality Needs. Reluctant managers are likely to have a high need for achievement but low need for power and affiliation. This low level of need for affiliation is perhaps most noticeable. They are likely to be high innovators, but because they have no interest in management, this shows only in their technical activities. They are also likely to be Type B personalities—that is, not very hard driving, time conscious, or people sensitive.

Management Style and Sanctions. Their management style is so easy going as to be almost nonexistent. Sanctions are rarely used, and when they are, it is usually through the removal of social contact.

How to Cope. The main problem with reluctant managers is getting them to engage in any interpersonal interactions at all. This, of course, has the advantage that you can get on with doing whatever it is you like doing. Indeed, you could almost take over the running of the department yourself, if that is what you want. Because of their dislike of social interaction and management, any request for advice on managerial matters is dealt with in whatever way is quickest. This is in accordance with the principle suggesting that we spend more time on jobs that we like. In these circumstances, it is probably best to use your control of information selectively. Present a number of alternatives from which the manager can choose, with your own preferred alternative strongly supported by evidence.

The Open Manager

This manager has a very firm belief in the value of participation and getting everyone involved. He or she holds regular meetings ad nauseam, to review progress and decide on future actions, as well as ad hoc gatherings of subgroups or the department as a whole to deal with issues as they arise. Most people appreciate this, but there is the feeling that, on occasion, too much time is spent ensuring that all involved are committed when such commitment is not really necessary.

Personality Needs. These people have little need for power, a high need for affiliation (supportive rather than assuring), and may have a high or low need for achievement. They are likely to be midrange between being innovative or adaptive in their approach to management issues. In addition, the open manager is usually flexible and in touch with his or her own behavioral needs.

Management Style and Sanctions. Such managers are highly participative and will use position and resource power only if and when required. They may also have some personal power and are admired by their subordinates.

How to Cope. There are very few problems in dealing with open managers, other than deciding how open you are going to be in return. The danger with being too open is that the information you divulge may be used to your disadvantage, either at another time or by other people. A related problem may be that the manager is open in situations that may not be appropriate—for example, in relations with other department personnel who are behaving politically.

Because the open manager engenders commitment, there is also a danger that you will become too involved and take more work on than is good for you. In these circumstances, you will need to say no. Many subordinates may find this difficult, and saying no in a positive way is a skill that must be learned.

Dealing With Colleagues

Relationships with colleagues at work are critical, not only to our productivity but also to our health and job satisfaction. Lazarus (1966) has found in his research that supportive social relationships with colleagues at work are less likely to create interpersonal pressures and will directly reduce levels of perceived job stress. Poor relationships between colleagues have been defined by University of Michigan researchers as "those which include low trust, low supportiveness, and low interest in listening and trying to deal with problems that confront the organizational member" (Caplan, Cobb, French, Van Harrison, & Pinneau, 1975). Indeed, their studies and others (Cooper & Payne, 1988) have concluded that mistrust between colleagues at work is related to high role ambiguity, poor communications, and very important, to competition between colleagues. As Bob Slocum says in Heller's (1975) *Something Happened,* "I always feel very secure and very superior when I'm sitting inside someone's office with the door closed and other people, perhaps Kagle, or Green or Brown, are doing all the worrying on the outside about what's going on, in the inside."

Dealing With Competitive and Threatened Colleagues

It is inevitable in organizations that there will be some element of competition between colleagues in an effort to get promotion, to avoid losing a job, or just to catch the eye of the boss. A certain degree of competition is healthy, but it also can cause distress, especially if it inhibits one's natural style of behavior. The following case study, from Watts and Cooper (1992), illustrates how colleague competition and avoidance coping strategy were counterproductive. Karen is a middle manager in a medium-sized company:

> Karen really wanted to do well at work but she realized that her male colleagues were threatened by her intellect. They were often sarcastic about her degree in business administration—"Call yourself an administrator and you can't make coffee without spilling it in the saucer"—one joke after another. They liked it best when she was joking and laughing with them and playing the dumb blonde, and she was very good at that. So long as she played the part, she remained popular. But if she attracted the attention of her boss with the speed and quality of her work, then the mockery would start in earnest. So Karen chose to avoid being a success. But she became deeply resentful about playing a role that was not hers. By avoiding success she kept the peace, but in "keeping the peace" she lost her own peace of mind.

It should be obvious from this example that avoidance as a strategy for dealing with competitive colleagues can be personally damaging and can increase anxiety levels. What is more productive is to recognize signs indicating that colleagues feel threatened and then identify potential sources of this threat. The following signals should alert you to threatened colleagues:

Signs of Threatened Colleagues

Covering up papers on his or her desk when you enter the room
Constantly opposing you at meetings when the boss is present

Hiding important files or materials from you

Undermining you with other colleagues or with the boss

Using memos as a means of conveying lack of trust in you

Noticeably excluding you from office and social functions

Animated conversations that turn to silence when you enter the room

Once you have identified that a colleague seems threatened or behaves in an excessively competitive manner, try to identify the reason. Is he or she threatened by your perceived competence, your interest in a particular senior job (which he or she also covets), the boss's relationship with you, or some personality or management style incompatibility? Only by identifying the source of the problem can you begin to decide on an appropriate strategy to deal with it. Every strategy chosen has its pluses and minuses. The solution or coping strategy with the most benefits or pluses and the fewest costs or minuses is the one that should be pursued.

In addition, an appropriate response to threatened colleagues requires a positive attitude on your part or what Jim and Jonathan Quick (1984) refer to as "constructive self-talk" or "positive mental monologue." This monologue, or self-talk, can range from being gently positive to harshly condemning. When people engage in negative self-talk, they achieve nothing and only maintain the stress, dissipating their emotional energies. If you are involved in constructive self-talk, it can achieve positive task outcomes and psychological results. Examples of what the Quicks suggest, in terms of "being positive," can be seen in Table 4.1.

All these constructive self-talks seek to turn bad experiences into potentially positive ones in our relationships with colleagues. They constitute thinking differently about stressful situations and therefore gaining some control. We don't have to be trapped in defensive or negative coping that can only make relationships and situations worse. We can make choices all the time. Watts and Cooper (1992) provide an example of one's options in circumstances involving a colleague: Suppose a workmate, who is known to "fiddle" the books and cheat his employers, is given a promotion and you are passed over. Which reaction do you choose?

- *Headbanger:* Furious anger at being treated this way. Take it out on others.

- *Pragmatist:*Accept that it is an unjust fact of life. Get on with your work.
- *Reformer:* Campaign for better decision making in the firm, involving consultation at shop-floor levels where there is better understanding of the workforce. Discuss your concerns in confidence with respected peers.
- *Alchemist:* Turn base metal into gold. Decide to turn this bad experience into a good one in any way possible. Equip yourself to cope when things do not go your way or get even worse. Make an informed decision to stay and be positive—or leave.

All of these reactions are possible options, or we might pass through them all in stages over a period of months. But to get stuck with the first option and never move on is a disastrous course of action.

Improving Customer and Client Relationships

Besides dealing with bosses and colleagues, many managers and staff members in organizations must cope with difficult or justifiably aggrieved customers and clients. As part of a total quality management (TQM) environment, many organizations recognize the importance of appropriately dealing with those who use our products or services. One large U.K. company has established the following quality standard procedure for dealing with customer complaints as part of its TQM program:

> If we all commit ourselves to quality and service there will be appreciably fewer occasions when our customers will need to complain, or indeed when we will need to complain to each other. But we do not live in a perfect world and occasionally we will be on the receiving end of complaints. At such times it will be important to
>
> Apologize sincerely.
>
> See the complaint as a second chance to impress the customer. Good recovery when things go wrong can sometimes bring greater accolades than if nothing had gone wrong in the first place.
>
> Listen and do not argue. Recognize and appreciate how the customer feels.

TABLE 4.1 Constructive Self-talk in Dealing With Difficult Colleagues at Work

Situation	Negative Mental Monologue	Constructive Self-Talk
Colleague hides important business file	"He's a nasty person, I'll just avoid him and hide material from him as well."	"I wonder why he is doing this. I will make an effort to get to know him."
Colleague always "puts you down" at meetings, especially when the boss is present	"I'll fight him at every turn, preparing myself with more damaging material to undermine him."	"I let myself get disturbed too much by this colleague, maybe something's bothering him. I'll see if I can find out what it is."
Memos sent to other colleagues highlighting one of your business mistakes	"If that's the game he wants to play, just watch my memos."	"Why did he need to send that memo. He must feel threatened by me. Have I done something to hurt him? How can I improve my relationship with him?"

Collect all data and details so you can fully understand what went wrong.

Accept responsibility; avoid passing the buck.

Avoid excuses; they are unlikely to be appreciated.

Find out what the customer wants; work out what you can do; and do it quickly.

If there are things you can't do, say so and explain why not.

Check that your action or promised action is acceptable to the customer and thank him or her for bringing the problem to your attention.

Work out what you can learn from the experience and how you can stop it from happening again.

Contact the customer at a later date to ensure that there has been no recurrence.

This approach recognizes the importance of adequately dealing with difficult or unhappy customers, using a set of guidelines based on some basic psychological concepts. Other techniques might employ transactional analysis (see later) to understand where customers or clients are "coming from."

DEALING WITH SEXUAL HARASSMENT

Jane is a single parent with two teenage children and the sole "breadwinner" in her family. She works in the laboratory of a large chemical company. Very ambitious, she has been attending college in the evening to attain more qualifications. She has always gotten along well with her boss and is very pleased when he asks her to attend a European conference with him. Over dinner on the last evening of the conference, he hints that there is a promotion coming up in the department and that Jane may be a potential candidate. A male colleague, Eric, is also a possible candidate. Although less able and less committed to his job than Jane, he has been with the company 6 months longer than Jane. Jane's boss suggests that he could "swing" the decision her way if she would sleep with him that night. Does she go along with him or say no and so risk losing her job and her only source of income?

Mary works as a motor mechanic. Her coworkers are male. The workplace walls are cluttered with sexually explicit posters and pictures. Frequently, the men make jokes and rude comments about Mary's physical attributes and appearance, comparing her with the women in the photographs. They clearly seem to think it's all a bit of harmless fun, but for Mary, it's no joking matter. She comes to dread going to work. She wants to leave but wonders if she will find things much the same in any other garage.

The preceding scenarios illustrate two types of sexual harassment:

- *Quid pro quo* harassment or sexual blackmail—one thing in return for another (Jane's experience)
- Environmental harassment—one's conduct creates hostility and harms the victim's working environment, even though no tangible employment benefits have been lost (Mary's experience)

The term *sexual harassment* is recent, having been coined in the 1970s. However, it is essentially a new label for an old problem; many women of earlier generations found themselves receiving unwanted sexual attention at work. Sexual harassment is not only demeaning, but as Jane's case clearly illustrates, it deprives women of opportunities that are available to men without sexual conditions. It is recognized that potential victims of sexual harassment are not exclusively female. Men, particularly homosexuals, ethnic minorities, or those working in predominantly female work environments, are also vulnerable to unwanted sexual attention. However, according to a recent U.K. survey (Phillips et al., 1989), women are 7 to 8 times more likely to experience sexual harassment than are men. Furthermore, whereas sexual harassment of males is generally confined to verbal abuse and suggestive remarks, women more commonly experience some form of physical contact. Therefore, this section will focus primarily on the problem of sexual harassment and its associated stress as it affects women. But much of the advice given will have equal application to men who may find themselves in this situation.

The evidence suggests that sexual harassment at work is a serious and growing problem. Rather than an "unexpected work event," sexual harassment in the workplace appears to be relatively commonplace. This may be a reflection of more enlightened social attitudes toward discussion of such a topic. It may also reflect growing numbers of women entering the workforce, especially in nontraditional work roles and occupations, and the difficulties or problems that such changes in status present in work environments.

Research Trends

One of the earliest surveys was conducted in the United States in 1976 by a popular women's magazine, *Redbook*. The results were staggering; 88% of 9,000 female respondents reported experiences of sexual harassment at work. A subsequent study, undertaken by the U.S. Merit Systems Protection Board (USMSPB, 1981) of 23,000 federal employees, found that 42% of the women surveyed had experienced some form of sexual harassment within a 2-year period (1978-1980). The USMSPB repeated its study in 1988 by sending a questionnaire to 13,000 federal employees. The results obtained were almost identical.

A number of generally smaller-scale U.K. studies have also produced some disturbing results. In 1981, the Liverpool branch of NALGO (National Association of Local Government Employees/Officers) surveyed its members and found that 55% of women had experienced sexual harassment, either in their current or in previous jobs (Equal Opportunities Working Party, 1981). Evidence from a study of women in West Yorkshire, sponsored by the Equal Opportunities Commission (1983), found that 59% of women had been sexually harassed. In 1987, the Labor Research Department's survey reported a figure of 73%. A similar figure was reported by the National Association of School Teachers Union of Women Teachers, who conducted a survey in Birmingham Secondary Schools in the same year. More recently, a survey of 1,000 workers in Britain (Phillips et al., 1989) comprised 800 women and 200 men; it revealed that 16% of women and 2% of men reported sexual harassment in their current jobs. In 1991, in a survey undertaken for the Alfred Marks Bureau of the employment agency's clients, 47% of women and 14% of men stated that they had been sexually harassed.

Similar studies conducted in various European countries suggest that the problem of sexual harassment is widespread and not culturally specific. For example, a survey of 4,200 secretaries in West Germany, conducted by *Brigette* magazine, reported that 54% had been sexually harassed. Another study, commissioned by the Netherlands Government and conducted by the University of Groningen (1986), found that 58% of women questioned had experienced sexual harassment at work.

Although these surveys appear to differ considerably in terms of their estimates of magnitude of the problem from 16% to 88%, these differences can be accounted for by a number of factors, including differences in sample sizes, differences in sampling techniques, differences in the questions asked (e.g., some surveys asked about experiences in current jobs; others asked about previous as well as current jobs), and the degree of consciousness of sexual harassment as a concept and awareness as to its constituent behaviors. For example, the United States was the first country to introduce administrative regulations and judicial recognition that sexual harassment is unlawful sex discrimination. One would expect, therefore, that individual Americans would have more heightened awareness of the concept than some European countries, where sexual harassment has not been thought of as falling within the intended scope of discrimination law. Nevertheless, despite the varying estimates, available evidence is sufficiently consistent to confirm that sexual harassment is a real and pervasive problem in the workplace.

The Impact of
Sexual Harassment

Sexual attraction between men and women often occurs where they work together. Provided that this attraction is mutual, with no abuse of power, the relationship may be distracting but is not necessarily a problem. The behaviors associated with sexual attraction, what has been called the "courting cues" (Cohen, 1983), may take the form of sexual innuendo, staring, unnecessary touching, patting, or other manifestations and may be similar to those behaviors that constitute sexual harassment. However, sexual harassment differs from sexual attraction in that harassment is unwelcome and unacceptable to the recipient. According to a report issued by the Commission of the European Communities (1988), "The essential feature of sexual harassment is that it is one-sided, uninvited or imposed."

There are many definitions of the kinds of behavior that may be described as sexual harassment. These fall into three broad categories—verbal, physical and visual—and include the conduct listed in Table 4.2.

However, it is obvious that merely producing a litany of behaviors that may be regarded as sexual harassment does not provide a clear definition of the term. Different women may regard the same conduct as tolerable or offensive. Individual women may regard the same conduct by different men differently. A woman may find it acceptable for a close male colleague to occasionally put his arm around her, but that does not give *all* the males she works with license to do the same. Therefore, whether or not a behavior constitutes sexual harassment is defined by the recipient's *response* rather than the *intention* of the perpetrator.

Despite the prevalence of sexual harassment at work, few women make any formal complaint. Indeed, many organizations still perceive sexual harassment as an individual rather than an organizational problem. Estimates are that as few as 1 in a 1,000 harassed women will file any formal complaint (Colatosi & Karg, 1992). Typically, reluctance to report an incident stems from fear of retaliation or fear of loss of privacy. Many victims also consider that to make any formal complaint is to be criticized and not taken seriously.

However, the outcomes of sexual harassment are far from trivial. As Kasinky (1972, quoted in Colatosi & Karg, 1992) puts it, "Sexual

TABLE 4.2 Categories of Sexual Harassment

Verbal Conduct	Physical Conduct	Visual Conduct
Propositions, requests, or demands for sexual favors	Staring or leering Gestures Unnecessary touching, patting, or pinching or brushing against another employee's body "Wolf" whistles	Displays of pornographic pictures or other sexually suggestive or derogatory objects, pictures, or written materials
Pressure for sexual activity Offensive flirtations Suggestive remarks Innuendos or lewd comments Tricks or jokes of a sexual nature Offensive comments about appearance or dress Derogatory or degrading abuse		

SOURCE: Commission of the European Communities (1988).

harassment may be one of the most widespread occupational health hazards women face, as well as the best guarded secret."

Response to sexual harassment is not dissimilar from response to rape. According to Jensen and Gutek (1983), surveyed victims of sexual harassment report having experienced disgust (80%), anger (68%), and depression (20%). Sexual harassment is associated with a range of negative outcomes, including deterioration in work performance, psychological and physical health, affective feelings toward one's job, and relationships with others at work (Crull, 1982; Gutek, 1985). For example, the USMSPB study (1981) found that one third of women who had been sexually harassed felt that their emotional or physical condition had been adversely affected by the experience. Crull (1982) found that 75% of victims reported a decrease in work performance, 90% reported a deterioration in psychological health, and 63% reported a deterioration in physical health.

Studies have shown that most women initially respond to sexual harassment either by ignoring the incident and doing nothing about it or by attempting to avoid the harasser. If the behavior persists and the working environment becomes intolerable and stressful, many women feel forced to leave the organization or ask for a transfer to another department. Crull (1982) reports that as many as 42% of the victims in her survey had resigned from jobs because of sexual harassment. A further 25% of those sampled had been fired or laid off as a result of sexual harassment.

Aside from the adverse impact this may have on the victim's career and self-image, such actions are costly to organizations. The USMSPB found that sexual harassment at work, in terms of recruitment and retraining costs alone to the federal government, amounted to $189 million over a 2-year period from May 1978 to May 1980. In a wider context, the sudden, and often ill-explained, decision to quit reinforces the stereotype of women as "unreliable" workers and negatively affects future career prospects.

Stopping Sexual Harassment

There are many possible responses to sexual harassment. Typically, these fall into two categories: actions that lead to a change in behavior in the harassed individual and actions that confront or attempt to change the behavior of the harasser.

Avoidance or Acting to Reduce Exposure to Risk. As discussed, the majority of victims of sexual harassment decide to remove themselves from the situation by leaving the organization or transferring to another department. Such behavior is usually preceded by attempts to avoid or ignore the harasser and staying "cool," hoping this person will get the message that the victim is not interested. Such tactics are usually unsuccessful, as evidenced by the number of women who ultimately feel forced to resign.

Sexual harassment requires quick action on the part of the victim. Otherwise, it does not go away but usually gets worse. Attempting to ignore rather than confront the offensive behavior can lead to misunderstanding and confusing messages. Passivity may be interpreted as acquiescence and encouragement rather than as rejection. It also may even work against the woman should she decide to file a formal complaint at some later date.

Alternatively, some individuals may respond by changing or altering aspects of themselves—their behavior, appearance, or way of dressing—because they feel that they may have inadvertently encouraged the harasser in some way by being overly friendly or too overtly "attractive." Again, this strategy will likely fail to deter the harasser and may serve only to fuel negative self-feelings within the victim. According to Philips (1989), 11% of victims consider themselves partly at fault by failing to be assertive or inadvertently encouraging comments or advances.

It has to be recognized that sexual harassment is not motivated by physical attraction or sexual desire but by the need for "power over"; male confusion about a woman's sex role, work role, and expected behavior; or both.

Dominant theories attribute sexual harassment as being (a) a result of unequal distribution of power between the sexes and therefore part of the "continuum of male-aggressive, female-passive patterns" (Medea & Thompson, 1974) or (b) the carryover into the workplace of gender-based expectations for behavior that are irrelevant or inappropriate to work, whereby a woman's work role is confused with her sex role. For example, a male boss may expect female subordinates to be pleased by his flirtatious comments and actions in the same way as a wife or girlfriend would be.

Consequently, the likelihood of being sexually harassed is more the outcome of a woman's status or role rather than of the way she looks or behaves and is unlikely to be deterred by any overt or deliberate suppression of sexuality. Hence, women in nontraditional occupations of low status in an organization (i.e., part-time workers), highly educated women, or women perceived to be more vulnerable because of their status in society generally as single parents, divorcees, widows, or ethnic minorities face an increased risk of sexual harassment (USMSPB, 1981).

Therefore, strategies that aim to avoid or reduce exposure to risk by changing behaviors of harassed individuals are mostly ineffective and often costly in both financial and humanistic terms. They not only fail to present a satisfactory solution to the harassed victim's continuing problem, they also allow perpetrators every chance to continue their offensive behavior.

Physical Reactions. Bart (1981) interviewed women who had been raped and those who had avoided rape and concluded that those who avoided rape were more likely to have screamed and physically struggled as opposed to talking or pleading. This would suggest that some form of physical reaction (i.e., a sharp slap, a shove away, or the removal of an offending hand) may stop any further advances. However, such actions are not without their dangers, especially if a victim is alone with the harasser. Also, as was found in the same study, physical responses often need to be augmented by other strategies.

Confrontation. Ignoring, giggling, smiling, disapproving frowns, or embarrassed looks, because they send mixed signals, are open to misinterpretation and usually are ineffective in stopping unwanted sexual advances. Ridiculing the harasser or making a joke of the incident may work sometimes, but making light of or appearing to trivialize the matter and so denying its seriousness may escalate a harasser's unwanted attentions or lead to retaliation. The more effective strategy requires a clear, consistent, and assertive response that leaves the perpetrator in no doubt that the behavior is unacceptable. Assertive responses include the following:

- Looking the harasser straight in the eyes
- Speaking in a firm and calm tone of voice
- Making a clear statement as to why the unwanted behavior is unacceptable and what you want the harasser to do or not to do

Colatosi and Karg (1992) suggest that positive commands—"I want you to keep your hands to yourself"—work better than negative commands—"I don't want you to touch me." Moreover, they suggest that it is useful to describe in words what is happening while it is happening (i.e., "You have your hand on my left breast; I want you to remove it *now!*") or to repeat aloud any sexual requests made.

- Telling the harasser what you propose to do if the behavior continues (e.g., file a formal complaint)

Internal Report. Externalizing, telling others about the incident, is preferable to ignoring it or pretending it never happened. Often, the victim is not the only target, and sharing information is an effective way in which to build up a case against the perpetrator. A group complaint is more powerful than that of a single victim. Telling, or enlisting help from, friends, coworkers, or a spouse helps in gathering support and advice that may make the victim feel better. But action to directly address and arrest the problem requires a formal report to a supervisor, manager, trade union representative, or other company official. If the harasser is one's boss, such reports should be made to that person's immediate superior. A decision to report should be made as soon as possible after the incident has occurred. The victim must record time, place, and specific details of the harassment and note if there were any witnesses. When the harasser is confronted, the first reaction will probably be denial. Thus, it is helpful for those investigating such incidents to be able to direct the discussion toward specific allegations separately. The victim should avoid procrastination. Evidence presented by Professor Anita Hill, in her recent case against U.S. Supreme Court nominee Clarence Thomas, was very much weakened by the fact that 10 years had elapsed before she made specific information public.

Many large organizations have incorporated policies and procedures relating to sexual harassment, but the absence of any formal policy should not deter a report. The climate concerning sexual harassment is considerably more sympathetic to victims than it was in the past. Many trade unions—for example, the Council of Civil Service Unions, the National Union of Public Employees, and the Amalgamated Engineering Union—provide awareness education, training, and guidelines to local union representatives about how to sensitively and effectively deal with reports of sexual harassment.

External Report. In a recent survey of more than 7,000 working women, conducted in Spain (UGT, 1987), it was found that 33% believed there was no legal remedy for sexual harassment, and 43% were unaware of a specific legal remedy or how to have recourse to it.

If harassment takes the form of sexual assault, the victim has remedies under criminal law and can report the matter to police. In the United Kingdom, as yet, there is no specific law relating to sexual harassment. However, cases have successfully been brought to court under provisions of the Sex Discrimination Act of 1975. The first sexual harassment case, *Strathclyde Regional Council vs. Porcelli,* came before Scottish courts in 1986. It involved sexual harassment by a woman's male colleagues, including suggestive remarks and brushing up against the complainant. Mrs. Porcelli's claim that such behavior constituted unlawful discrimination, on the grounds that because of her gender she had been treated unfavorably, was upheld and an award of £3,000 was made in her favor against her employer. Besides cases prosecuted under the Sex Discrimination Act, sexual harassment, if it results in resignation or dismissal, has been recognized as valid grounds for claiming unfair or constructive dismissal under §55(2)(c) of the Employment Protection (Consolidation) Act. Such actions, if successful, result in an award for damages against the organization, not against the perpetrator. Advice concerning legal action is available from the Equal Opportunities Commission.

Other external agencies offer help to victims of sexual harassment. Women Against Sexual Harassment (WASH)[1] provides free and confidential advice to anyone who has been sexually harassed at work. In addition to general legal and employment advice, it will also provide support and counseling. Support and counseling are also available from local rape crisis centers. The emotional response to sexual harassment is often similar to that following rape, and trained rape counselors can be extremely helpful in helping women work through these negative emotions.

Choosing the Right Option

The decision to take legal action should probably be regarded as a "weapon of last resort." Legal proceedings are likely to be lengthy and contested but, if successful, may result in eventual reinstatement, financial award for damages, or both. The major disadvantage is that, at present, such hearings are public, and the anticipation of a court appearance is itself likely to be stressful. Although effective solutions for sexual harassment are unlikely to be achieved without the incentive of avoiding legal sanctions (Rubenstein, 1988), other options are best pursued at the outset.

Confrontation is the most effective initial option, for a variety of reasons:

1. It communicates a clear message that the behavior is unacceptable and not to be repeated.
2. If the act was motivated by power, confronting and challenging it upsets the traditional continuum of aggressive-male, passive-female behavior pattern. The disequilibrium this creates is likely to be shocking. In behaving assertively, a victim is likely to feel more confident and in control of the situation and may be perceived by the harasser as less vulnerable and powerless, particularly if the woman

makes it clear that she will not hesitate to take "official" action if the behavior continues.

3. Alternatively, if the offense resulted from inappropriate male expectations of the female role in the workplace, or role confusion, then it directly confronts this issue and creates an opportunity for role clarification and negotiation. Often, only by confrontation can a woman create an atmosphere within which she can feel comfortable in stating exactly what she does, or does not, find to be acceptable work-related behavior. For example, a female engineer who finds herself at the receiving end of suggestive comments might wish to restate and remind her male colleagues of certain facts: She is employed as an engineer and not as a woman; therefore, she expects them to limit their comments to business-related issues.

Popovich and Licata (1987) suggest that role negotiation techniques (RNT) can be useful, decreasing the opportunity for a person's sex role and work role to become confused and thereby prevent sexual harassment. Such techniques should be periodically employed in organizations before any incident occurs. One technique involves each member of a work group listing, often anonymously, what he or she feels the other members should do more of or do better, what to do less of, and what to change. These comments then form a basis for group negotiation, and a final written contract is then drawn up detailing work roles and expectations of group members. Periodic checks can then be made on the role-set members via appraisals.

Whether a victim decides to take further action and make a formal report of the incident will depend on the particular circumstances. However, it is in this person's best interests to keep a private record of the incident and perhaps informally report it to a colleague. Any recurrence, then, should automatically be confronted and formally reported through internal channels.

In more general terms, action can be taken by individuals within organizations to address potential problems of sexual harassment in the workplace by lobbying for the introduction of formal policies and procedures and for the provision of awareness and education training programs. Assertiveness training can also be extremely helpful in developing personal skills for coping with such attacks and handling the power dynamics of the workplace more generally.

COPING WITH UNETHICAL BEHAVIOR
IN THE WORKPLACE

"The world only goes forward because of those who oppose it."

—Goethe

In a recent survey (Burke, Maddock, & Rose, 1993), 43% of senior managers and professionals considered that being unfaithful to one's domestic partner was morally worse than tax fraud. Only 20% thought tax fraud was morally worse than partner infidelity. It is not the debate as to the relative moral superiority of these two acts that is interesting but that these findings illustrate how individuals are even willing to engage in such a debate, thereby confirming their discrimination between codes of behavior and ethics appropriate to personal life and those appropriate to business matters.

The issue of business ethics has fueled considerable recent controversy. Events such as the tragedy at Bhopal, the Exxon oil spill in Alaska, the Guinness affair, the BCCI fraud, and the Maxwell pension fund scandal have raised the question as to whether "business ethics" and "profit maximization" are oxymoronic. Certainly, business language equates its activities with game playing. There are major players, winners and losers, and mavericks, and often, those reputed to bend the rules or "bluff" and get away with it seem to receive the respect of other players. Consistent with the sporting analogy, those who draw attention to unethical practices or shout "foul play" are described as whistle-blowers, implying that they stop the action and spoil the fun. Frequently, whistle-blowers in business games emerge, like their sporting equivalent on the playing field, as the least popular individuals in the organization. Underlying this analogy is the "conscience comforter" that, if business is merely a game and the most important goal is to win, then winning by any means is justified.

It has been argued that unethical behavior is often a result of organizational culture, in terms of pressure that managers sometimes feel for performance measured solely in economic and competitive terms. However, not all immoral behavior in the workplace is directed toward improving organizational performance; some is more concerned with lining individual pockets or with self-protection.

Thomas McCann tells how, in the early 1950s, the management of America's United Fruit Company helped overthrow the Guatemalan government to improve local business conditions. McCann, an employee at the time, was aware of this decision and yet did nothing about it. He was so closely involved with the company that he did not consider this decision a moral or ethical issue. Because he did not recognize the event as a moral dilemma, it did not cause him stress at the time, but the fact that he has since openly talked about the issue presumably suggests that, retrospectively, his earlier behavior caused him some discomfort.

Relatively few individuals are likely to find themselves in situations in which the questionable behavior of members of their organization has such potentially dramatic consequences. However, more commonly, we may be asked to do something, or have knowledge that others intend to or have done something, that offends our moral values and sense of right and wrong. Such situations might involve lying on behalf of a colleague or boss, discovering a colleague fiddling his or her expenses, or knowingly engaging in practices that endanger the health of other workers or customers.

Whether or not an individual decides to compromise his or her values and go along with such behavior depends on several things:

- An assessment of the level of personal responsibility: the classic, "I had no choice; I was only obeying orders" excuse

- An estimation of potential harm, as opposed to benefits, of such action: For example, "If I lie on behalf of my boss, I will feel really bad and it is likely that I will be asked to tell more serious lies in the future" versus "If I lie on behalf of my boss, nothing really awful will happen and he or she will act favorably toward me in the future"

- An expectation of discovery and punishment

In an organizational setting, because there is greater anonymity and the risks and consequences attached to any action are often less immediate, more diffuse, and indirect, moral boundaries are less clear-cut and more fuzzy. Consequently, individuals are more likely to adopt double standards and to behave in ways that they would never consider right and proper in the conduct of their personal lives.

Research has consistently demonstrated that individuals behave differently when in a group or organizational situation. Compared with individuals working alone, groups are more likely to make relatively risky and extreme decisions. The pressure on one to yield and conform to the perception of the majority view is often considerable, particularly if the other group members have higher status in the organization. Responsibility for action is more diffused in a group, and the sense of personal responsibility is reduced.

Moral or ethical dilemmas in the workplace are notably problematic and potentially stressful. Often, workers are likely to feel as if they are "between a rock and a hard place." If they decide to turn a blind eye or go along with the situation, the resultant incongruence between personal and organizational values is likely to cause distress. The alternative is also distressing, in that any decision to challenge group behavior may result in job loss or amount to career suicide.

Nielson (1987) suggests a number of possible courses of action that managers can pursue in such situations:

- Not think about it
- Go along and get along
- Protest
- Conscientiously object
- Leave
- Secretly blow the whistle (leak documents, write anonymously to superiors, etc.)
- Publicly blow the whistle
- Secretly threaten to blow the whistle
- Engage in sabotage
- Negotiate and build consensus for change

These strategies vary in terms of degree to which they are likely to be effective and the amount of personal risk involved.

Not Thinking or Going Along. Obviously, such strategies do nothing to stop unethical behavior in working situations and are more likely to promote its continuance. In the short term, one may be able to "switch off" or rationalize his or her behavior; however, there may be long-term detrimental psychological consequences. Behaving unethically or passively condoning such activity may end in dismissal or legal action. This is the situation with the *Daily Mirror* board of directors, who now face being sued by the Maxwell Pension Fund holders.

Protesting and Conscientiously Objecting. Depending on the seriousness and scale of the situation, speaking out and letting people know how you feel may feel good; this is preferable to keeping quiet and bottling things up. But protests of outrage and indignation alone may simply be disregarded or amount to career suicide. A quiet word in the ear of a colleague who is cheating on expenses may be enough to cause that person to rethink the illicit actions. However, the lone voice of a more junior employee attacking major corporate policies or aspects of organizational behavior is unlikely to gain serious or sympathetic hearing and carries considerable personal risk.

Leaving. Leaving represents the ultimate protest. Probably very few people can afford, financially or psychologically, or will have the moral courage to perform the heroic act of resigning on a matter of principle. Furthermore, leaving the organization is unlikely to cause it to change its ways.

Blowing the Whistle. Any decision to secretly blow the whistle has definite advantages over doing so publicly, because there is less fear of retaliation, although certainly, such an action will precipitate some form of internal inquiry or "witch-hunt." Secretly blowing the whistle has the disadvantage that it often makes the individual feel sneaky, and the person lives in perpetual fear of being found out. The same applies to acts of sabotage. Another course, going public, will likely have the most impact. But to do so, the individual may first have to leave the organization. Before doing so, one should also seek legal advice to ascertain whether he or she is likely to be in breach of any employment contract.

According to Nielsen (1987), secretly threatening to blow the whistle is often a more effective strategy. It has the advantage of giving the individual or the organization time to reconsider and change the behavior. It is also less risky to the potential whistle-blower, and if it works successfully, this ploy is unlikely to result in retaliation or any self-recrimination.

Negotiate and Build Consensus for Change. This differs from protesting and objecting in that one seeks to confront the unethical behavior, but at the same time it offers a solution or alternative course of action.

For example, colleagues who resort to expense account fraud (a) may be underpaid, (b) may have large debts, or (c) may think it is "legitimate" to make a little bit extra out of their employer—everybody does it! Depending on circumstances, it may be appropriate to suggest to them that they speak to their boss, that they seek financial advice and support, or that such excuses are not valid. The implicit question is, What would happen if everybody did the same? Another possibility is to work toward introducing more stringent controls and procedures.

Choosing the Right Course of Action. Negotiation and building consensus for change are likely to be effective and, at the same time, create the least personal risk to the person seeking change. However, there are circumstances in which negotiation may fail. In any ethical dilemma, it is important to work through internal channels first before going public. Any complaints should be based on documented evidence, not on rumor or hearsay, and be put in writing whenever possible. In addition, whistle-blowers should try to get the support of other colleagues or union representatives.

It is also important not only for these individuals to stay on their best work behavior but also to make sure that their information is correct and appropriately presented. Before making any formal complaint or report, it is advisable to speak informally with a senior colleague whom one trusts. Such dialogues can help clarify issues. On issues of major policy—for example, environmental issues—one may be unable to alter organizational thinking overnight, but directing energy into local action groups may not only salve one's conscience, such indirect pressure may ultimately bring about needed change.

IMPROVING COMMUNICATION WITHIN THE WORK ENVIRONMENT

"When I use a word," Humpty Dumpty said in rather a scornful tone, "it means just what I choose it to mean—neither more nor less."

—Lewis Carroll, *Alice in Wonderland*

Poor communication or lack of it, whether at work or at home, can be an important source, a manifestation, or a consequence of stress.

As will be discussed in more detail in the next chapter, one of the major sources found for stress among acquired or merged employees was poor communication. Similarly, when employees experience high levels of stress, there is a tendency to withdraw, to communicate less effectively, or to distort communication.

The effectiveness of workplace communication can be realistically measured only in terms of relative dissatisfaction, given that it is an area of organizational activity that employees must constantly strive to improve. Nobody is ever totally or always happy with the amount, frequency, or level of information he or she receives, even those at the most senior levels of a company.

Communication is a vast subject that can never be adequately covered in a volume as slim as this. Virtually every hassle we have discussed or will discuss in this book touches on this issue of communication. In this short section, we have chosen to focus on one particular communication theory—transactional analysis—that we consider useful for improving workplace interpersonal communication. In outlining this theory and its implications, we will draw heavily on the work of Cox and Cox (1980).

Transactional Analysis

The theory of transactional analysis (TA) was originally developed by Eric Berne in 1961. It is a set of concepts that provide comprehensive and useful ways of analyzing how people relate and interact with each other. In TA terms, these interactions are termed *transactions.*

According to TA theory, each individual possesses three "ego states," or consistent patterns of feelings and experiences giving rise to a corresponding pattern of behavior (see Figure 4.1). The three ego states are these:

■ The *Parent* ego state is a storehouse of significant other's attitudes, feelings, and ways of behaving. It provides us with our values, opinions, social consciences, rules, and regulations. The Parent has three main functions: (a) active giving of care and support (the Nurturing Parent), (b) caring use of prohibition to protect and sustain (the Critical or Controlling Parent), and (c) provision of limits and stan-

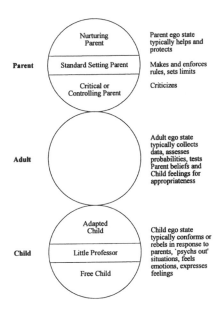

Figure 4.1. Personality Structure: The Three Ego States
SOURCE: Cox and Cox (1980).

dards (the Standard-Setting Parent). A person acting from the Parent ego state is doing so according to his or system of values.

■ The *Adult* ego state is an unemotional, rational ego state. It is that part of the person that collects and processes information and events in an objective way, weighs alternatives, tests reality, and makes decisions based on present and past experience. When a person acts from the Adult ego state, he or she operates free of strong feelings.

■ The *Child* ego state is a collection of childhood experiences, feelings, reactions, and decisions. It is the source of energy and of natural emotions and behaviors. There are three kinds of child behaviors: (a) spontaneous, natural responses (the Free Child); (b) responses determined by social pressures and norms (the Adapted Child); and (c) intuitive, problem-solving behavior (the Little Professor). A person whose strong feelings are triggered is operating from the Child ego state.

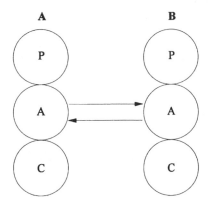

A   `What time is the meeting?'

B   `Four o'clock'

Figure 4.2. Example of a Parallel Transaction, Adult to Adult

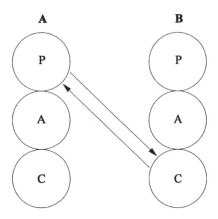

A   `You look worried. Do you need some help?'
(Parent to Child)

B   `Yes, please, I don't know how to structure this
report.'
(Child to Parent)

Figure 4.3. Example of a Complementary Transaction, Nurturing
Parent to Child

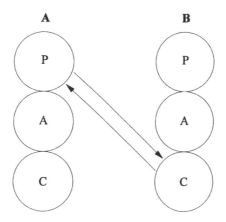

| A | 'You've got these files in a right mess. Sort them out.' (Parent to Child) |
| B | 'Yes, I'll do it right away.' (Child to Parent) |

Figure 4.4. Example of a Complementary Transaction, Critical Parent to Child

The Transaction. A transaction is a unit of social interaction; a series of transactions forms a conversation. During a transaction, a message originates in one person's ego state and is "sent" to a particular state of another person. If the other person responds from the ego state addressed (i.e., there is a parallel or complementary transaction), then communication between the two parties will be experienced as satisfactory and the conversation may continue indefinitely (see Figures 4.2, 4.3, and 4.4).

Problems occur in transactions when a person receives a response from an ego state other than the one addressed. This is termed a *crossed transaction.* The effect is to stop any dialogue, even though this may be only momentarily. The other person may then have to readjust and move from one ego state to another to satisfactorily continue the dialogue. If he or she doesn't, the communication will be experienced as unsatisfactory and may develop into conflict (see Figure 4.5).

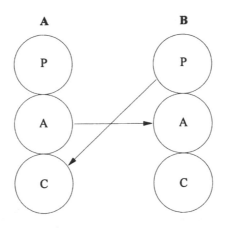

A	'Where are the latest sales figures?'
	(Adult to Adult)

B	'I don't know, you're always losing things.'
	(Critical Parent to Child)

Figure 4.5. Example of a Crossed Transaction

Sometimes there are *ulterior transactions.* According to Cox and Cox (1980), "These occur when there is an overt courteous 'social' transaction (what is seen and heard out loud) and at the same time, a covert 'psychological' transaction which may or may not be experienced consciously by the person involved." If there is an ulterior transaction, attention will be paid to the covert level, whether this is in awareness or not. It is not uncommon for people to report after a conversation that they were vaguely aware that "something else was going on" (see Figure 4.6).

Transactional analysis provides a useful way of analyzing interactions between organizational members. For example, most criticism is usually directed from the Critical or Controlling Parent and expects a reply from the Adapted Child. In other words, the critic expects the person receiving the criticism to passively accept it and respond contritely. In reality, what usually happens is the person being criticized either responds rebelliously from the Free Child or retaliates

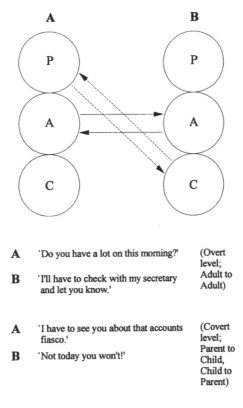

| A | 'Do you have a lot on this morning?' | (Overt level; |
| B | 'I'll have to check with my secretary and let you know.' | Adult to Adult) |

| A | 'I have to see you about that accounts fiasco.' | (Covert level; |
| B | 'Not today you won't!' | Parent to Child, Child to Parent) |

Figure 4.6. Example of an Ulterior Transaction

from the Critical or Controlling Parent. Consequently, the criticism becomes destructive or is ignored. The criticism is likely to be constructive if the transaction is parallel, from Adult to Adult because it will be unemotionally focused on specific acts, issues, and behaviors rather than on personalities.

NOTE

1. Women Against Sexual Harassment (WASH), 242 Pentonville Road, London, N1 9UN.

MANAGING EVERYDAY STRESSFUL EVENTS

A lot of the problems we encounter both at work and in our personal lives are ones that we create ourselves. Typically, such problems occur because we failed to manage our time effectively; were unable to say "no" and agreed to do something we didn't want to do or were unable to do in the time available; or totally mishandled a situation, upset others, lost control, or got angry. Frequently, the outcome of such situations causes stress and anxiety and leaves us feeling bad or inadequate.

In this section, we focus on the numerous hassles that we are all likely to encounter during a day at work—hassles that emanate primarily from our desk or work situation. Individually, these hassles may often appear trivial or insignificant to those around us and when related to others frequently sound more like "moans" than problems. However, their cumulative effect is often stressful, and they represent the type of hassles that can be overcome and resolved only by personal action. We will begin with *travel,* a major source of hassle that starts before we even get to work. Then, we will move on to discuss *time management, interruptions,* and *managing workload.*

TRAVEL STRESS

"Travelling is the ruin of all happiness."

Fanny Burney, 1833-1898

7:30 a.m.	The day starts badly. You forgot to set the alarm and you're running late. You have an important client meeting at 9:30 a.m., and you intended to get into the office early to reread the papers in preparation for the meeting. You have to stop for gas on the way in, which further delays you. Traffic is heavy and there is roadwork on the highway. You find yourself in a line of slow-moving traffic, and it's at least 4 miles until the next exit. As you're crawling along, you suddenly become aware that you have developed a flat tire. You limp onto the shoulder of the road and look at your watch; it's 8:50 a.m., and you're still some 8 miles from your office. You're not going to make that meeting! What do you do?
Typical and ineffective response	You sit there fuming, then get out of the car and kick the tire. Mentally, you set yourself up for a hassle-packed day by telling yourself, "What a bloody awful day this has turned out to be. . . . Why did *I* have to get a flat tire today of all days?"
Effective stress-reducing response	You take a deep breath, calmly get out of the car, and proceed to change the tire. Rather than letting the situation wind you up by ascribing an inanimate object, such as the tire, with the intelligence and malicious intent to develop a flat deliberately to delay you, you accept that although the timing is unfortunate, these things happen. As soon as you can, you call your office and explain the delay. You also ask your secretary to check your calendar for the day and try to put back or rearrange any later appointments. You ask yourself if there is anything you have learned from the experience that could reduce the likelihood of its happening again.

After the weather, travel and its associated difficulties would probably rate as the second most popular topic of conversation among the U.K. population. Getting from one place to another, whatever the mode of transportation selected, often presents a major hassle. A multitude of factors can potentially go wrong on any journey (and invariably do). Poor weather conditions; traffic congestion; roadwork; breakdowns; missed connections; long, often uninformed, periods spent waiting around at stations and airport terminals; and jet lag all contrive to make travel a potentially exhausting and stressful experience. Travel, it has been said, broadens the mind; it is equally true that it can also blow the mind! Everyday work stress often begins before the individual has even reached the workplace.

Many studies have demonstrated that travel is stress inducing and impairs job performance. For example, travelers crossing time zones at a rapid pace experience problems similar to those of shift workers—for example, disturbed sleep and increased fatigue (Akersted, 1985). However, the focus of these studies has tended to be on travel as an occupation (e.g., pilots, bus drivers) rather than on travel as a further dimension of work life more generally. However, one has only to spend a short time observing the behavior of fellow travelers in an airport terminal or in a traffic jam to recognize that one has entered a stressful environment.

Coping With Travel Stress

Car Travel

In a recent, yet unpublished, survey of more than 120 senior U.K. executives, it was found that although the car, not surprisingly, given its convenience and flexibility, was the most usual and most preferred mode of travel within the United Kingdom, it was also considered to be the most stressful. The executives considered that car journeys lasting in excess of 2.5 hours impaired their subsequent work performance. Apart from any subsequent effect on job performance, stress severely impairs driving behavior in adversely affecting concentration and decision-making abilities. Drivers under stress are more likely to take risks, misjudge the speed of others, or inaccurately estimate size and distance. Consequently, human factors play a major role in road accidents. According to the Department of Transport,[1] in the United Kingdom less than 6% of motor accidents can be accounted for by road and/or vehicle conditions alone. Obviously, it is difficult to isolate whether travel is the primary causal source of stress or further exacerbates existing stress levels.

However, clear evidence as to the link between stress and accident involvement has emerged from a recent study of over 100 company car drivers (Cartwright, Cooper, & Barron, 1993). It was found that over a 3-year period, drivers who were involved in accidents had significantly higher stress levels than did their accident-free colleagues. Interestingly, accident involvement was found to be little influenced by driver age. Overall, the study also found that an important factor in predicting accident involvement was the extent to which individuals exercised time management skills as a means of coping with stress. In other words, the "better" or more developed the time management skills of the individual, the fewer accidents that person incurred. This is because effective time managers are more likely to allow "contingency time" when planning journeys and arranging work schedules and so are less likely to find themselves driving under "time-urgent" conditions, which make them more prone to be careless and make mistakes.

Some organizations, such as Mobil Oil, ICI, and Shell U.K., run programs and issue guidelines to help their managers avoid or more effectively cope with travel stress. ICI maintains that the organization has more fatalities through driving accidents than industrial incidents. Their advice to managers is to avoid travel whenever possible and to make fuller use of telephone and video conference facilities. If a journey is necessary, they suggest that where reasonably practicable, rail or air services should be used in preference to travel by road. In addition, the following advice is likely to be useful:

In Preparation

■ Always allow contingency time when planning a journey, even if the journey is relatively short. Check out your route before you leave if you are traveling to unfamiliar areas. If possible, consult with others who make the journey regularly.

■ Carry out regular maintenance checks on your vehicle. Discipline yourself to fill up with gas, check oil, check tire pressures, and the like on your way home rather than leaving it until the morning, particularly if you have an early start, because many garages do not open before 8:00 a.m. Attending a basic car maintenance class can prove useful. Many local police stations organize special evenings for female drivers that provide basic car maintenance skills and advice on personal security.

■ One of the major sources of stress associated with travel delays is the inability to contact others. Always carry spare change for parking meters and phone boxes, together with a phone card in the glove box. Car phones are invaluable when experiencing travel difficulties. If used with discretion (i.e., switched off when necessary), they can greatly alleviate travel stress. Of particular potential benefit to female travelers, many of the large motoring organizations in the United Kingdom will fit direct telephone helpline links relatively inexpensively. These enable the driver to summon help in the event of a breakdown; these organizations will also inform family and others of your delay.

■ Do not be overzealous in the planning of your work schedules. Meetings invariably overrun rather than finish early.

In the scenario we presented at the beginning of this section, some advance planning and time management skills may have helped alleviate some stress, but what can one do to reduce anxiety during the course of travel, particularly if you find yourself stuck in traffic or waiting around for the tow truck.

While Traveling

■ Take time to ensure that your seat is adjusted to a position that provides a comfortable body posture and that your mirrors are in a position that provide you with good visibility without straining your neck. Such points should also be borne in mind when purchasing a vehicle. Many Japanese cars, for example, were not ergonomically designed for drivers over 6 feet tall, although many have or are taking action to rectify this.

■ When driving in slow-moving traffic or when stationary, regularly perform simple relaxation techniques to reduce body tension; the neck, shoulders, and hands are particularly vulnerable areas. Helen Froggatt and Paul Stamp (1991) suggest the following exercise routine:

For the neck
Slowly turn your head from side to side; then gently nod the head
   up and down.

For the shoulders
Raise the shoulders gently to your ears. Hold and then let go. Relax by feeling the weight of the arms pulling down.

For the hands
Spread the fingers, stretch them out, and relax. Then clench them into a fist and relax. Repeat this exercise several times.

■ There are several relaxation tapes on the market specifically designed for use when driving. When selecting a relaxation tape, make sure that you listen to at least part of it before buying. For such tapes to achieve their objective, you must feel comfortable with the voice of the presenter; otherwise, it will irritate rather than relax. Alternatively, you may wish to compile a tape of your own favorite pieces of music that have a calming and relaxing effect on you personally.

■ Vary your speed to avoid fatigue. On long journeys, stop and take a short break to stretch your legs every hour and a half. Many highway accidents occur because the driver momentarily nodded off; hot or poorly ventilated cars can induce fatigue.

■ Traffic delays and other travel holdups are particularly frustrating because they are events that are out of the individual's control. Aggressively thumping the steering wheel, cursing, and sighing serve no useful purpose other than to heighten anxiety. Nothing can alter the fact that you are going to be late, so calm down, take deep breaths, and find a more productive way of passing the time. Because it is recognized that Japanese drivers typically spend a considerable amount of time traveling short distances in heavily congested urban areas, manufacturers built into their cars a much wider range of sound systems and other gadgets than have their European counterparts. These are deliberately intended to "amuse" and occupy drivers while in standing traffic. With some advance thought, it should be possible to usefully occupy time should a delay occur—for example, catching up on correspondence, making notes on a minidictaphone, always carrying a "reading" file, or using the time to learn a foreign language.

Rail and Air Travel

Much of the previous advice similarly applies to rail and air travel; however, here are a few additional tips:

■ Rail and air travel can provide a useful opportunity to catch up on sleep and arrive at one's destination alert and ready for business. Investment in a portable stereo or personal cassette player can provide an alternative means of replacing the facilities provided by the car stereo and can be used to play relaxation tapes to aid sleep. On certain long-haul flights, some carriers now incorporate relaxation programs into their in-flight entertainment systems.

■ Many airlines provide general guidelines for air travelers. In particular, it is recommended that passengers limit their alcohol intake and wear loose-fitting, comfortable clothes while traveling. Although alcohol may temporarily have a soporific effect, like coffee, it can actually interfere with sleep.

■ It is recognized by airlines that the effects of jet lag and its disturbance to the body's circadian rhythm on performance can be potentially disastrous. Precise scientific formulas are used to calculate the necessary amount of rest time their personnel must take before resuming duty. The effects of long-distance travel across time zones are particularly pronounced in the afternoon and early evening after a westbound flight, which is about the time the individual would normally have expected to rest. The speed of adjustment varies among individuals, but recovery is generally faster after westbound than after eastbound flights.

Mobil Oil advises its executives that 1 day per time zone crossed should be taken to recover naturally. For eastbound flights, they suggest taking a night flight in order to arrive the following morning, staying awake until midmorning, then taking a nap of no more than 2 hours and afterward remaining awake until normal bedtime. On westbound flights, individuals are advised to stay awake on arrival and not go to bed until local time. Herbal teas and herbally derived sedatives can be useful in aiding sleep on initial arrival.

MANAGING TIME

"All my possessions for a moment of time."

—Queen Elizabeth I's last words

Assuming a typical response to the previous scenario, the day might continue as follows:

9:45 a.m.	You eventually arrive at your office. You go to collect the file for the client meeting, and the phone rings. A subordinate is having some problems accessing information on the computer; brusquely you give hasty instructions. You then spend a further 10 minutes wading through the few huge piles of paper stacked on your desk, searching for the right file. You notice a new pile of correspondence and phone messages on the desk; some marked urgent. You contemplate dealing with these, but you're now already 30 minutes late for this meeting. Suddenly, you remember that before you left last night your boss popped in and suggested a meeting at 10:30 a.m. You're going to be late for that one too!
Typical and ineffective response	When an individual finds oneself in this situation, there is a strong temptation to cut one's losses, go home "sick," and abandon the day all together, working on the premise that things are bound to get worse rather than better. One is reminded of the image of John Cleese as the head teacher in the film *Clockwise* hurtling uncontrollably, yet predictably, from one disaster to another, with an imaginary key in his back which winds tighter and tighter, increasing his stress level as he confronts each situation.
Stress-reducing response	Ignore the mail, but quickly scan the urgent telephone messages. Delegate or get someone to phone back to let people know when you will be able to contact them. Have your meeting with your boss rearranged. Take a deep breath, relax, and calmly go to the meeting.
	Having taken the sting out of your immediate problems, you've bought yourself some time so you can focus all your attention on the meeting. Resolve to take time out to reorganize your desk as soon as possible—and do it! On your return, check that everything is OK with that computing problem—it could result in repercussions.

Time, like money, is a limited resource that can be used to good or bad effect. However, although it is possible to make more money, unfortunately you can't knit more time—there can be only 24 hours in a day. The inability to manage time effectively is often a major source of stress. Although self-imposed time pressure can stimulate action, constantly working under time pressures over which we perceive ourselves to have little or no control—situations that we experience as demanding action yet give no time to think—are unlikely to result in good performance. Although we may blame others for wasting our time, the biggest culprit is usually ourselves. Time wasters fall into the following categories.

The Mañanas

Individuals who fall into this category cause themselves problems because they procrastinate, preferring to think about work rather than doing it. When things move on their desk, the things don't leave it but, rather, they change location. Habitually, such individuals postpone decisions so that, consequently, tomorrow always becomes the busiest day of the week. When challenged, they invariably offer excuses rather than reasons for not having done something. Although they frequently complain about interruptions, they actually often encourage them so that they can procrastinate even more.

Procrastination often stems from boredom, a lack of confidence, or reluctance to seek clarification. As a result, indecision becomes the safest option. Individuals also procrastinate when they are overwhelmed by work demands and are unable to prioritize the tasks in hand. Here are some basic tips to effective time management:

- Break up overwhelming tasks into smaller jobs. Set a deadline for completing the entire task and work on it a little bit everyday.
- Draw up a "to do" list of all the tasks you need to complete in the short term (i.e., within the next week), the midterm (i.e., the next month) and the long term. Then each day, draw up a list of things that you need "to do today." Regularly review your "to do" lists and incorporate items on to your daily lists. Prioritize each task in terms of its urgency and importance. If you have difficulty prioritizing tasks, ask other interested parties to help. If you have agreed about your priorities with your boss, he or she can hardly blame you if a non-priority item does not get completed today!
- When planning your work schedule, attempt to balance routine tasks with the more enjoyable jobs. It is a good idea to begin the day with an enjoyable job; then the sense of achievement will set you in a positive frame of mind for the rest of the day.
- Combat paper shuffling by resolving to handle each piece of paper only once. Read it, act on it, file it, or throw it away.

■ Accept that risks are inevitable and that no decisions are ever made on the basis of complete information. Set a time limit, gather as much information as possible, and make a decision.

The Poor Delegators

Individuals who fall into this category waste a considerable amount of their time doing work that could easily and more effectively have been done by somebody else. Typically, this is because they lack trust in others, are trying to impress others, fear confrontation, or lack the ability to say "no" and so take on too much. Poor delegators tend to expect perfection in themselves and others and often have difficulty separating the trivial from the important. If they do delegate, they worry and fuss and are unable to stand back, frequently "checking up" on others and changing instructions. Their interfering behavior and overt lack of confidence in others' abilities are often major sources of frustration to those with whom they work, and characteristically, work relationships can be poor. They are prone to openly complain about the performance of colleagues and subordinates, yet they allow them little opportunity to develop. Rather than impressing their superiors by their indispensability, poor delegators often find themselves doing the same job for years, because they have failed in their own self-development and those around them. They should consider the following:

■ Delegation does not mean abdication. Although initially, it may take time to explain or train another person to take on a new task, in the long term, that investment will reap dividends.

■ Always take time out to explain exactly what is required; poor delegators are often also poor communicators, which is why they are frequently disappointed with the efforts of others. Check at the time that the other person is clear about what he or she needs to do and ask if that person anticipates any problems. Be specific as to when you require the task to be completed and indicate that he or she can come back to you for help or information.

■ Having delegated a job, leave the person to get on with it. If you knew that someone was going to check *everything you did*, would you do it as well?

■ As soon as you become aware that a deadline is unrealistic, renegotiate, delegate, or let someone know. People are less upset and can readjust better if they are told sometime in advance that their initial expectations are not going to be met rather than at the last minute.

■ Avoid taking on unnecessary work that does not fulfill your objectives or that could be done by others by your learning to say "no" politely and assertively. Practice, saying it aloud in front of a mirror.

The Disorganized

Individuals who fall into this category are instantly recognizable by the mounds of paper that form barricades around their desks. Disorganized individuals frequently miss or are late for appointments. When they do arrive, they have often forgotten or misplaced their papers and spend the first 10 or 15 minutes paper shuffling in an attempt to catch up on what is going on. A large part of their day is spent in "hide-and-seek" type activities: hunting for car keys, scraps of papers, cigarette packets with vital phone numbers on them, and so on.

Psychologically, disorganized individuals perceive their problems as stemming from work overload; they erect these barricades of files around their desk as a defense against the onslaught of further work. Although outwardly they give the impression of being immensely busy, they actually achieve very little. Furthermore, they tend to waste other people's time, regularly rechecking details and instructions because they have failed to initially record such information accurately or have misplaced their notes.

Typically, such individuals subscribe to the view that creative minds are rarely tidy, rather than to the more logical and likely outcome that a cluttered desk reflects a cluttered mind. Disorganized individuals are often anxious that their work contribution will not be recognized or are fearful that if they make things too easy for others to follow, this will in some way devalue their worth and may make their position vulnerable.

Here are some helpful hints for the disorganized:

■ Remember that it takes time to plan effectively to save time. Setting up a system; color coding files for easier identification; and investing in a yearly planner chart, filofax, and so on to improve organization and allow you to regain control of your chaos all play dividends in the long term.

■ Discipline yourself to do the filing every day.

■ Make out a "to do" list regularly at the start of each day and review it each evening. Clear the top of your desk and put everything out of sight except for the task you are currently working on. Keep your "in" tray somewhere else—for example, on the top of a filing cabinet rather than on your desk. Then you will not be overwhelmed and demotivated by the amount of work you have to do.

■ Stick to one task and finish it!

■ Invest in a large hardbacked "scribbler" pad for recording all your notes, messages, and the like in *one place,* making a note of the date and action you have to take. Photocopy only material sufficient for your needs; avoid making multiple copies for "safety." Avoid spontaneous use of the telephone.

■ Think before you telephone, draw up a list of *all* the information you require from the caller. This will avoid the necessity to call someone back several times as you become aware of further information you need as you work through the task. The opening and closing courtesies of telephone calls all take up time. This will also save your time waiting for others to phone you back with information and you will be able to progress the task without interruption.

■ Identify your prime time for working, when your energy levels are high, for the complex tasks and save the trivial routine tasks for nonprime time. Most people tend to be either "larks" (i.e., at their best in the mornings) or "night owls" (i.e., at their best in the late afternoons and evenings). Research evidence suggests that larks tend to be more introvert and owls more extrovert personalities.

■ Try to "batch" phone calls or group trivial or routine tasks and tackle them as one task.

■ When making an appointment in your diary, enter a finish time as well as a start time. Allocate time exclusively to yourself—to think, to plan, to write that urgent report. Don't fill up all your available time with meetings. Just because there is a space on your calendar does not mean that you are doing nothing and therefore that this time can automatically be committed to others.

The Mushrooms

Individuals who fall into this category are usually unclear about the purposes, aims, and objectives of what they are required to do.

Rather like the mañanas, they speculate and inwardly question what they should do rather than doing it. Frequently, they expend a great deal of effort performing jobs that are unnecessary, do not match task requirements, or duplicate the work of others. Often, they also waste time "reinventing the wheel." Typically, such individuals waste time because they are nonassertive, contemplating what action is required and remaining uninformed and "in the dark" rather than speaking out and seeking clarification. Consequently, they frequently encounter difficulties in prioritizing, and their behavior can easily be interpreted by others as being apathetic.

Individuals who remain mushrooms are likely to quickly become job dissatisfied. Because their problem is basically a lack of assertion and communication skills, they are likely to benefit from interpersonal skills development courses. Many organizations run assertion training courses. Alternatively, many community colleges and continuing education departments of universities also run short courses in this area. Although there are a number of good books on the subject (e.g., *Assertiveness: A Positive Process* by C. Beals, B. Hopson, & M. Scally, 1991; *Developing Assertiveness* by Anni Townend, 1991), the key to developing assertiveness is to practice, practice, practice; the opportunity to practice techniques in role-play activities in a learning environment is extremely important. Fundamental to assertive behavior is the individual's acceptance of rights for her- or himself and responsibilities to others. Items 6 and 7 in the following list are of particular relevance to "mushrooms":

1. I have the right to express my thoughts and opinions, even though they may be different from those of others.
2. I have the right to express my feelings and take responsibility for them.
3. I have the right to say "yes" to people.
4. I have the right to change my mind without making excuses.
5. I have the right to make mistakes and to be responsible for them.
6. I have the right to say "I don't know."
7. I have the right to say "I don't understand."
8. I have the right to ask for what I want.
9. I have the right to say "no" without feeling guilty.
10. I have the right to be respected by others and to respect them.
11. I have the right to be listened to and taken seriously.

12. I have the right to be independent.

13. I have the right to be successful.

14. I have the right to choose not to assert myself.
(Adapted from Beals, Hopson & Scally, 1991; Townend, 1991)

MANAGING INTERRUPTIONS

12:25 p.m.
Having survived the client meeting and made it through a rocky meeting with your disgruntled boss, who was clearly not impressed with your timekeeping, you arrive back at your desk. By skipping lunch, you may be able to salvage something of the day and so turn your attention to that report that has to be finished today and that you planned to start 2 hours ago. You settle down to it, but you never get more than two sentences written before you are interrupted by the phone or somebody dropping by your office. Before you know it, it's 3:00 p.m. and you're still struggling with the first page. At this rate, you're going to be home late yet again tonight, and it's your 6-year-old's school concert . . .

Typical and ineffective response
You continue to battle through the interruptions and resign yourself to staying on late until the report is finished and to missing your child's concert, despite the inevitable row at home that will occur as a result. You produce a report with which you are far from satisfied and either take it home with you to rewrite over a bottle of whisky or worry about it all night.

Stress-reducing response
First, you take a short half-hour lunch break and get some fresh air. Then you cocoon yourself in your office or move to an alternative quieter location and create an interruption-free environment for a hour or two and focus all your attention on the report. Consequently, you are able to finish the report by 4:00 p.m. and still have time to attend to your waiting phone messages and other matters, organize yourself for the morning and leave on time.

It has been estimated that 1 hour of concentrated work is worth 4 hours of interrupted time. Interruptions take up time in themselves, but they also disturb concentration so that having dealt with interruption, it then takes the individual further time to refocus on the original task. Telephone calls and casual "droppers by" are the two major sources of interruptions.

The Telephone

Batching phone calls, planning what you are going to say or need to know in advance, and deliberately disciplining yourself to place a specific time limit on the length of a phone call are useful techniques for managing the telephone more effectively. It is good practice to aim to limit telephone calls to 3 minutes. An egg timer by your phone is a useful device for doing this. If the volume and complexity of the information you wish to convey is likely to take more than 3 minutes to transmit, then there are more appropriate means of communication available to you, which are potentially less ambiguous and open to misunderstanding than the phone (e.g., electronic mail, fax machine, letter). They also have the advantage of providing an exact and permanent record of the communication for future reference. Because many phone calls need to be reconfirmed in writing at some later point in time, a decision from the outset to use such alternative methods avoids unnecessary duplication of effort and time. It is also sound practice to check at the outset whether the person you are calling has time to speak to ensure that you have his or her full attention. Develop the skill of terminating a call on an action point. When making a difficult call that requires a positive and assertive approach, handle the call "standing up"; this will help to reinforce your assertive behavior and improve voice projection. However, although such tactics are useful in limiting interruptions and using time more effectively, there are circumstances that because of their time urgency or demands for creativity, it is necessary to get away from interruptions. In such circumstances, call-diversion facilities and answering machines provide the solution. By way of an experiment, North Western Mutual Life, an American insurance company, introduced a "quiet hour" for their employees during which all incoming calls were blocked and dealt with by the switchboard. Operators took messages that were then relayed to employees at the end of the hour. The scheme proved extremely successful. In 1 year, the organization reported a 23% rise in productivity.

Casual "Droppers By"

Although being interrupted can provide a welcome diversionary break from a boring or tedious task, too many interruptions during the course of the day are a waste of time, distracting, and irritating. For many years, fragmentation has been recognized to be a key feature of a manager's typical working day. The role of the manager is highly interactive. It has been estimated that, typically, a manager will engage in more than 100 brief interactions in the course of a day. Consequently, he or she will rarely work for more than 30 minutes on any one item. To some extent, the problem of interruptions has increased over the years as managers have been encouraged to be more accessible to their staff and to adopt an open-door managerial style. Furthermore, changing attitudes toward work organization, the demands of new technology, and monetary pressure to use space more efficiently have meant that open-plan offices, first introduced in the 1960s, have increasingly become the norm. The debate concerning the relative merits of traditional versus open-plan offices still continues. A study of clerical employees in the United States (Oldham, 1985), found that employees experienced more difficulty in focusing on the task, felt less able to effectively communicate privately with others, and were generally less satisfied with an open-plan layout than with more traditional partitioned offices. Therefore, although at general and social levels, open-plan offices may make it easier for individuals to interact, the lack of privacy and increased likelihood of interruptions suggests that organizations also need to provide quiet areas or designated rooms where employees can meet in private or occasionally work on tasks requiring uninterrupted concentration.

There are a variety of strategies for controlling interruptions:

■ Establish quiet hours during which you can work undisturbed. This may mean closing your door and putting a notice outside. In open-plan offices, this is obviously not possible; although, it is the practice in some organizations to encourage employees to indicate when they do not want to be disturbed. One such organization issues employees a flagholder and two flags, one green, the other red. Employees place the green flag at the front corner of their desk when they are working on everyday tasks and can be interrupted. Employees display the red flag when they are working on difficult and complex assignments and do not wish to be disturbed. Provided such indicators are used sensibly, they are likely to be respected by others and so can be effective in circumventing some of the problems of working in open-plan offices.

■ If possible, establish visiting hours when you are available for drop-in visitors and let people know when these are. Fix a definite time with others when you will answer their queries or review progress on a task rather than leaving it open-ended.

■ Whenever possible, arrange meetings away from your desk or office; this enables you to take control and leave when you want to.

■ Do not think that it is necessary to always preface and end an interaction with an obligatory amount of "small talk"; a pleasant smile will often suffice.

■ Do not hesitate in curbing wafflers by asking them to make their main point(s). If necessary interrupt them.

■ Do not invite casual droppers in to sit down; this will encourage them to stay longer.

■ When unexpectedly interrupted, ask the person how much time he or she needs, and if you haven't got it, explain that and make arrangements to see that person at an alternative time. If you only have 10 minutes, tell him or her and be prepared to keep the conversation to that length of time. There is no need to feel guilty—you kept your side of the bargain. Pointedly looking at one's watch can be an effective strategy in getting people to come to the point or to recognize that you are busy and need to get on.

■ When it comes to interrupting others, practice what you preach. Think twice before you interrupt somebody else. Do you genuinely need that person's input or are you just too lazy to think for yourself?

Avoid the automatic knee-jerk reaction to pick up the phone or walk over to somebody's desk by preparing a list of the information you need to give or ask, add to it as you work through the day, and then see that person once. Ask people if it is convenient to interrupt them and be sensitive and respectful of their time.

Finally, recognize that interruptions occur for a number of reasons: The person involved may (a) want to exchange information; (b) need reassurance or clarification about what he or she is doing; (c) be too lazy or lack the confidence to think alone (it is easier and less risky to be told what to do than to think it through for oneself); (d) want a casual chat to pass the time because he or she is bored, hasn't enough work to do, or needs the social contact; (e) want to talk to you about something else, perhaps of a personal nature, but doesn't know how to initiate the discussion and so keeps finding some other pretext to interrupt you.

Identifying the reason for the interruption can help guide the strategy for handling the situation and may indicate the need to change one's own behavior or managerial style. For example, if you find yourself constantly interrupted by requests for further information and clarification, this may suggest that your instructions are generally inadequate or poorly communicated. Often, taking time out to comprehensively brief colleagues or subordinates from the outset and encouraging them to ask questions and raise potentially difficult issues can avoid a steady flow of subsequent interruptions. Similarly, the constant referral of trivial or minor decisions may indicate that you are creating or nurturing an overdependent relationship between yourself and others. As previously discussed, this may be because you are a poor delegator. Alternatively, it may be that people are frightened of you or that you are "too available" and so may need to take action to sever the "umbilical cord."

MANAGING WORKLOAD: WORKING TO LIVE OR LIVING TO WORK

> *"I don't want to achieve immortality through my work—I want to achieve it by not dying."*
>
> —Woody Allen, *The Oxford Book of Quotations*

The impact of increased economic competition in recent years has led to substantial redundancies, downsizing, and delayering within organizations. The organizational model of the 1990s is frequently described as fitter, leaner, and more hungry than its predecessor. Leaner and more hungry it may be, but whether it is fitter remains open to debate. Fewer people doing the same amount of or more work means increased individual workloads and longer working hours. Meeting budget or exceeding productivity targets one year invariably has the result that, in real terms, budgets are cut and higher targets are set for the following year; working hard and meeting deadlines soon comes to mean working harder to meet even tighter deadlines the next time around.

It is therefore not surprising that work overload is one of the most commonly cited sources of workplace stress. There are two different types of work overload. *Quantitative* overload refers simply to having too much work to do. *Qualitative* overload refers to work that is too difficult for an individual. Quantitative overload often leads to working longer hours. The number of hours worked is a significant factor in employee health. A U.S. study of light industrial workers found that individuals under 45 years of age who worked more than 48 hours a week had twice the risk of death from coronary heart disease as did similar individuals working a maximum of 40 hours a week (Breslow & Buell, 1960). Long working hours can also create conflict and resentment at home and affect the quality of time spent with family, which can lead to marital difficulties.

For many in managerial jobs, working long hours, either because of the perceived demands of the workload or because the culture of the organization dictates that working late is symbolic of an executive's commitment, has increasingly become the norm. Although the average weekly hours worked by blue-collar and manual workers has decreased over time as a result of industrial legislation, white-collar working hours have actually increased. For many managers, a 10-hour working day is not uncommon, despite mounting research evidence that working beyond 40 hours a week results in time spent that is increasingly unproductive.

Working women are particularly vulnerable to overload. Women often find themselves taking on too much work, on the belief that they have to be seen to be good at their jobs or better than male colleagues in similar positions if they are to gain promotion. Furthermore, it is still the case that the bulk of the domestic chores and responsibilities of home, child care arrangements, and the like fall onto the shoulders of the working woman rather than on her male partner. The demands of these multiple roles—worker, mother, wife—mean that working women effectively have *two* jobs and can work as many hours at home as they do at the office or factory. Maintaining the "superwoman" image has health costs. In addition, at a time when male smoking behavior has been steadily decreasing, smoking among females has altered little, and in some age groups has actually increased. Research has demonstrated that the incidence of coronary heart disease among working mothers rises as the size of the family increases, whereas up to a certain limit, the reverse appears to apply to mothers who remain at home.

Too Much Work or Personal Inefficiency

If work overload is a major source of distress, then either you are not working effectively or you genuinely have too much work and need help from others. One way of systematically tackling the problem is to analyze how effectively you are working by keeping a time log for a week or two. To audit your time, divide each day into 15-minute segments; then at the end of each hour, make a note of the activities you were involved in and how long you spent on them. At the end of each day, record the total hours worked during that day. Such details could be recorded in a desk diary or on a separate sheet of paper. John Adair (1982), in his book, *Effective Time Management*, suggests the list of symbols shown in Table 5.1 as useful in recording managerial activities.

According to your profession or job, you may wish to devise your own set of symbols. For example, a university lecturer might include headings such as lecture preparation, marking, teaching, tutorials, research, pastoral care, and meetings. A general practitioner might use these headings: seeing patients, seeing medical representatives, writing reports, accounts and budgeting, home visits, practice meetings, reading journals.

At the end of the week, this data can then be summarized to identify the hours spent and the percentage of total time used under key headings. This will help you to identify *whether* and *where* you are wasting time—that is, the items that take up significant or unnecessary portions of your time but contribute nothing to your productivity—as well as areas where you could be better organized or perhaps delegate more. If the problem does lie in this area, it may be appropriate to reread the earlier sections of this chapter.

However, if the problem genuinely appears to be one of qualitative or quantitative overload, the time log will provide you with specific information that will help you present your case to others and negotiate for extra help. Initiating regular work group meetings to discuss current workload and task priorities, particularly if your workload emanates from several different sources, can be useful in gaining the support of others and sharing the workload.

TABLE 5.1 Symbols for Recording Time Spent in Managerial Activities

Code	Activities	Notes (Time Spent)
C	Committees: Any prearranged group meeting with or without an agenda	
I	Interviews: Any prearranged conversation, formal or informal, with a purpose	
D	Discussion: Talking not classified under C and I	
E	Education: Participating in lectures, training courses, conferences, and seminars	
F	Figure work: Working with numbers (budgets, invoices, etc.)	
P	On the telephone	
S	Dictating	
W	Writing	
J	Inspection: A personal tour of the workplace, walking the job	
Q	Traveling (and not doing other work listed above)	
T	Thinking	
O	Others: Specify what these activities are	

SOURCE: Adair (1982).

Taking on Too Much

As discussed earlier, the problem of workload can also stem from an inability to say "no" or poor delegation skills. Because we all tend to want to be liked by others, we often find it difficult to refuse requests because we fear our refusal may upset others or because we find it hard to say "no" without feeling guilty. Our need to please others and the feelings of guilt and selfishness we experience when we assert our wishes are often a product of early childhood and cultural upbringing. Parents and teachers tend to reward the compliant rather than the challenging child. We soon learn that we are likely to be praised for doing what others want us to and punished for being strong willed. This is particularly true for females, who are still generally socially conditioned to be acquiescent. Gender stereotyping remains pervasive in society, with different behavioral expectations for males and females: Boys shout and act aggressively, but girls are expected and encouraged to be quiet, passive, and cooperative.

Christian teaching carries many messages that encourage compliance and self-sacrifice. Examples include sayings such as, "The meek shall inherit the earth" or teachings that extol the virtue of putting up with an intolerable or unpleasant situation by "turning the other cheek." These childhood and other cultural messages, particularly those that still reinforce the concept of social class, such as "respecting one's betters," "knowing one's place," and so on, serve to reinforce attitudes of inferiority toward those with wealth, privilege, education, and authority and are very powerful in shaping adult behavior.

Thomas Harris (1969), in his book *I'm Okay—You're Okay: A Practical Guide to Transactional Analysis*, describes four fundamental life positions, as in Box 5.1.

I'm Okay—You're Okay. People who hold the "I'm okay—you're okay" viewpoint, see themselves as interdependent with others and their environment. Messages from others confirming that they are okay are appreciated and accepted, but these messages are not essential to their feelings of self-worth. Such individuals feel confident and comfortable with who they are and what they are. They do not see themselves as perfect but as okay. Because they realize that self-esteem is an individual responsibility, they find it easy to see and respond to others as okay, too. If they have a problem, they do not hesitate to approach others and express it assertively. Because they see others as being okay, they expect that others will also be reasonable and responsive, and when this attitude is conveyed, people usually are!

I'm Okay—You're Not Okay. People who hold this life position consider that the only person they can rely on is themselves. From their viewpoint, other people are worthless and potential enemies, and life would be fine if other people would just leave them alone. Everything bad that happens to them is somebody else's fault. Anything good is because of their own merits. When they have problems at work, they are often unwilling to speak out but, instead, inwardly fume and get angry or complain to others. They consider it pointless

I'm okay You're okay	I'm not okay You're okay
I'm okay You're not okay	I'm not okay You're not okay

Box 5.1.
SOURCE: Adapted from Harris (1969).

to speak out because they have already made up their minds that nothing will come of it.

I'm Not Okay—You're Okay. People who hold the "I'm not okay—you're okay" viewpoint believe that they are inferior to others. If they have problems at work, it is because they are to blame, either because they are incompetent or they lack sufficient influence to be able to change things.

I'm Not Okay—You're Not Okay. People who hold this life position consider that they are worthless and so is everybody else. They feel disconnected from others and their environment and have little motivation to try to overcome their negative feelings.

The concept of life positions is based on the theory that early in life, individuals adopt a fundamental belief about their own self-worth and that of others. According to Harris (1969), this position may be determined as early as 3 years of age. Although the "I'm okay—you're okay" life position is the healthiest, most individuals, albeit unconsciously, take up one of the other three positions. Harris argues that people achieve the "I'm okay—you're okay" approach only by challenging their assumptions and consciously choosing to move to this life position.

The theory of life positions is worth considering seriously because it plays a major role in determining how we communicate and respond to others in our daily lives. Adopting the "I'm okay—you're okay" life position is a fundamental precursor to assertive behavior and effective delegation in the workplace.

Problems of work overload can be solved with good assertion and delegation skills. If an individual keeps accepting more and more work, then one can be fairly certain that that person will be given more and more work. If one individual is able to dump work onto others and they accept it without overt objection, then that individual will be encouraged to repeat that behavior. If your boss continually passes more and more of his or her workload on to you, this solves a problem for your boss. Most bosses tend to perceive their roles as seeking solutions, not looking for problems. If you are unwilling to speak out about the problems this may cause you, you can hardly expect your boss to recognize your problems. It is important to tackle overload problems early before they escalate. People with too much work to do are more likely to make mistakes or miss deadlines. It is an unfortunate truth that although we are unlikely to get praised for the things that we do, we are almost certainly bound to be reprimanded or remembered for the things that we don't.

Some Other Ways of Improving Personal Efficiency

■ Some careful thought about the physical arrangement of your work space can improve your efficiency and combat fatigue. Have a comfortable and supportive chair and, perhaps, an amusing and/or relaxing poster or print that you can look at to pick you up or "escape" to at difficult times during the day. If you are fortunate enough to be able to choose the decor of your work environment, select colors and furnishings with which you feel comfortable. When choosing color schemes and furnishings for the home, we all tend to consider such details to be important and take time making that choice. Yet many of us actually spend more time in our offices than we do in our sitting rooms at home.

■ If you do a lot of writing and you are right-handed, you should position your desk so that the source of daylight should come from the left.

■ Working hard is not the same as working long hours. Creating "sanity breaks" during the day, occasional changes of scenery (i.e., taking walks) and changing the layout of your work space can be refreshing and stimulate creativity. Holidays are important: Arrange your work around your holidays, not your holidays around your work. If you do the latter, then you are likely to find that you never have sufficient space in your calendar to take any holidays. Book well in advance, pay for it, and go! Regular, short weekend or midweek breaks can often be as refreshing as the more usual 2-week periods, especially if you plan these for after busy work periods or outside traditional holiday times (i.e. autumn, winter), when most people are in need of an "pick-me-up."

■ Invest in labor- and time-saving devices at home (e.g., dishwashers) to lessen your workload. Delegate jobs at home to others in the family and share the workload. Working women, because they often feel guilty about the time they spend outside of the home, tend to overcompensate by continuing to do everything in the home themselves. Perhaps because their own mothers were not in paid employment outside the home and so they lack any realistic and appropriate role model, many women often also feel guilty about employing outside help. They may even feel that paying others, usually other women, to do chores such as the cleaning and ironing in some way exploits their own gender. Such feelings of guilt are misplaced and should be strongly fought and overcome. If you have one full-time and demanding job, then it is you who is being exploited, by yourself and by your family, if you take on another full-time job at home.

■ Finally, remember the principle of creativity and the creative process. There are four stages in the creative cycle: *preparation* (information collection), *incubation* (idea generation), *illumination* (solution recognition), and *verification* (solution adaptation). Having collected information in the preparation stage, the next stage, the incubation of ideas, is critical. According to Wallas (1926), an expert on creativity, incubation refers to the time that the individual is not consciously thinking about the problem but nevertheless is making some progress toward its solution as ideas first encountered during preparation are maturing. The implications are that when faced with a complex or novel problem, impulsively seizing on the first solution that comes to mind may not necessarily be the best course of action. Allowing a period of incubation, putting aside the problem for an hour or two, perhaps sleeping on it, is likely to produce a better outcome. Although not still in conscious thought, the brain effectively never switches off but continues unconsciously to work on the problem comparatively free of conscious constraints. Nina Catterton of the University of Virginia has studied the physiological differences in the body's response when it is under stress compared to being in a state of deep relaxation. She has found that under circumstances of peak arousal, the brain produces fewer creative beta waves, whereas when in a state of deep relaxation, more creative alpha or theta brain waves are produced. When people under immense pressure or stress report that "they are just not able to think clearly," this is not exclusively a subjective expression of their current feelings but is the manifestation of a physiological change in body functioning.

Admitting Inadequacies – Being Normal, Not Perfect

Nobody likes making mistakes or admitting that he or she can't cope, yet we all make mistakes or find ourselves in situations that we feel unable to resolve. Research has actually shown that although we tend to admire people who are capable and competent, we actually prefer people who, at the same time, we perceive also to be fallible. An American psychologist, Aronson, and his colleagues, (cited in Gross, 1987) in 1966 demonstrated this point by playing tape recordings of a program called *Quizbowl* (the U.S. equivalent of the British *University Challenge*) to a variety of people and asking them to rate how much they liked the contestants. The two superior contestants, who answered 92% of the questions correctly, were rated as more likable than the average performers. However, of these two, the one who was unfortunate enough to spill his coffee during the shows was the most liked. Another example, of how "human error," of appearing less than perfect, may actually enhance other's opinion of us is cited by the evidence of researchers Rubin and McNeil (1983). In an opinion poll taken immediately after President Kennedy had approved the ill-fated Bay of Pigs invasion of Cuba in 1961, the President's popularity was found to have actually increased as a result.

Telling others that you are having trouble coping or seeking advice is not an admission of weakness; it is smart problem-solving behavior. Most people, when asked for advice or help, are more likely to feel flattered and important rather than to view the suppliant as stupid or inadequate. Everyone likes to feel that he or she is regarded as some kind of "expert" in some field or another, particularly if the request for help or information is phrased in a way that makes one feel good—for example, "I feel that you are probably the best person to be able to help me. I'm having a problem with . . .," or "I'm having a problem with X. I think I would benefit from your experience in this area."

We all tend to be very good at seeing ways in which others could improve their performance or manage their lives better, but unless they ask us directly, we can be reluctant to offer that advice. Making a decision to ask advice of others can release a previously untapped resource of information that can help manage a situation better—and one always still has the option of ignoring it!

Individuals often avoid admitting mistakes—not only because they are fearful that others will think less of them as a result but because they wish to avoid criticism. Criticism can be extremely helpful provided that it focuses on facts, issues, and behavior rather than on personality and that it provides some guidance and direction as to how the individual might do things better in the future. It is important when giving and receiving criticism not to become defensive or aggressive because the situation will then easily escalate into conflict. If someone criticizes you, ask him or her to specify exactly what about your performance needs improving and how you should go about improving it. Such a strategy will encourage helpful criticism and exhaust unhelpful or manipulative criticism.

MANAGING MEETINGS

Attending meetings has become a key feature of organizational life. It is estimated that managers in large organizations typically spend 22% of their time at their desk and a massive 69% of their time in meetings. The overt purpose of any meeting is to make decisions and circulate information. Psychologists have long argued that group decision making results in greater acceptance and commitment to the decision. However, although this may be the case if the meeting is well managed and the group genuinely works together to reach true consensus, many meetings are time wasting and unproductive and result in conflict and ill feeling among members.

There are three levels to any group discussion:

1. The meeting has an explicit task or agenda.
2. It has established conventions governing the way in which social interaction between members is expected to be conducted through the operation of everyday courtesies.

3. There is a more covert emotional level at which feelings such as fear, insecurity, and aggression make themselves felt. Consequently many meetings have what is called a "hidden agenda."

Many of the problems associated with meetings arise at this third level. Hours can be devoted to elaborate game playing between members or discussion of a wide variety of red herrings that detract from the original purpose of the meeting. Game playing occurs with such frequency that one suspects that for many people the true purpose of any meeting is exactly that—to play games and make mischief. Meetings, therefore, become an exercise in role-playing. Descriptions of the most common roles played in meetings follow (Cooper, Makin, & Cox, 1989).

The Chair. The most formal role is that of chair. He or she is in a position to set the agenda, and a good chairman will keep the meeting running on time and to the point. Sadly, chairing a meeting well is an art that many people in this position lack. Often, this is because they are ill-prepared or unassertive and allow certain individuals to dominate the proceedings or digress from the agenda. Consequently, rather than controlling the meeting, they allow other informal role players to gain the upper hand and control them.

The Constant Talker. Chief of these is the constant talker who just loves to hear the sound of his or her own voice. It is often a man whose criteria of success is determined by the percentage of the total conversation he can dominate. Sometimes the constant talker also combines the role of the self-appointed comedian. The self-appointed comedian is unable to distinguish between informal and flippant behavior. Consequently, he or she constantly throws in humorous comments and may even embark on an epic "funny story" that bores everyone. The constant talker attends meetings only to speak, rarely to listen, and although that person may have experience of everything, he or she is often the expert on nothing.

The Anal Retentive Type. Another key role is what Freud would have called the anal retentive type. Often a prolific note taker, he or she insists on clear definitions and constantly seeks clarification, tending to refer back to earlier points throughout the discussion. The anal retentive person is the one who must "dot the i's and cross the t's " and who bores everybody present with his or her pedantic attention to detail, with the exception of fellow anal retentives, who admire that person's thoroughness.

The "Can't Do" Type. Then there are the "can't do" types, the people who always find reasons why something can't be done, usually based on some minor technical problem. This is the person who will point out, for example, that you can't have the annual general meeting on that day because he or she happens to know that some other (usually insignificant) meeting is taking place on the same day.

The "can't do" types are cunning, wanting to maintain the status quo. Because they have often been in the organization for a long time, they frequently quote historical experience as a ploy to block change: "It won't work; we tried that in 1964, and it was a disaster." When they are not challenging others with the "it won't work" dialogue, they sit silently, eyebrows raised, shaking their head.

A more subtle version of the "can't do" type, the "yes, but . . ." has emerged recently. They have learned about the need to sound positive, but they still can't bear to have things changed.

The Red Herring Types. These are the people who love meetings and want them to continue until 5:30 p.m. or beyond. Irrelevant issues are their specialty. They are also fairly cunning and *need* to call or attend meetings either to avoid work or to justify their lack of performance or simply because they do not have enough to do.

The Counterdependents. The red herring lovers are joined by the "counterdependents," those who usually disagree with everything, particularly if it comes from the chair or through consensus from the group. These people need to fight authority in whatever form but are usually so obvious in their disruptive behavior that a smart chairperson or group can easily marginalize them.

Other roles played at meetings are the "regular attender," "the social worker" (who resolves emotional conflicts between group members), "the whispering smartass," "the nonparticipating cynic," "the fence sitter," and of course, the "silent" type. The latter is present in all groups, and most other members project onto them lofty motives or objectives, such as "They are above this juvenile exercise," or "They will speak only if they have something significant to say." Usually, the silent type is shy, insecure, or just plain bored.

There are also common ploys or games that are played at meetings.

"Hey, Look at Me!" An individual ploy is attracting attention. Meetings give ambitious combatants an arena to compete in front of the boss, a kind of civilized forum for corporate gladiators to perform before the organizational princes and emperors. Meetings can also provide attenders with a sense of identification of their status and power. In this case, managers arrange meetings as a means of communicating to others the boundaries of their exclusive club—who is "in" and who is not.

Mark McCormack, of International Management Group, got so fed up with staff members wanting to be included in meetings that he set up a formal companywide one. Its purpose was not to discuss company business but simply to make everyone feel good because they were all invited. Everyone got the point.

"I Thought of It First!" A popular game is appropriating someone else's suggestions. Someone, usually junior or female, makes an interesting suggestion early in the meeting that is not picked up. Much later, the game is played, usually by some other more senior figure who propounds the idea as his or her own. The suggestion is, of course, identified with the player rather than the initiator.

"You Can Play Mom!" Another increasingly common game, as more women enter the world of work, is casting the woman in the role of secretary or Mom. The game is usually initiated by someone who is threatened by an overzealous or extremely competent female colleague. The purpose of this game is to deprofessionalize the woman, by forcing her into a traditional role of minute taker or coffee dispenser or sending her out of the meeting to copy any documents that may be required. By inveigling the female colleague to appear in a less serious or professional role, the player feels less challenged by her.

"Shopping a Colleague." Another game is SAC—shopping a colleague. This game takes many different forms, such as to point out

that a particular individual's contribution is irrelevant, because that was discussed at the previous meeting at which he or she was not present, or by excluding from the agenda someone's particular achievements. Alternatively, it may involve subtly letting it be known in a meeting that X was not at an "important meeting or conference" or implying that the player has a particularly close and confidential relationship with the individual's boss; so whenever X makes a suggestion, the player puts it down by saying, "That won't wash with your director. I *know* he was very much against the idea when we spoke recently." The list of SAC game plans is endless.

"Well, I Think That About Covers It." Because so many meetings end in confusion and without a decision, another more communal game is played at the end of the meetings, called "reaching a false consensus." It couches its so-called decision in such a vague way that a number of interpretations are possible. Everyone is happy, having spent the time productively. The reality is that the decision is so ambiguous that it is never acted on, or if it is, there is continuing internecine conflict, for which another meeting is necessary, to the absolute delight of the red herring types and the regular attenders.

In summary, for many, meetings provide the opportunity for social intercourse, to engage in battle in front of the boss, to avoid unpleasant or unsatisfying work, and to highlight social status and identity. It would seem that they are in fact a necessary, although not necessarily productive, psychological sideshow. But what then can be done to make meetings more productive? Apart from recognizing the roles and games that are being played and taking steps to minimize the disruption they may cause, the following tips are also useful:

Tips for a Better Meeting

■ First of all, before you call a meeting, consider whether the meeting is really necessary. How long should it be? Who should be there? When and where should it be held? Many people become regular attenders at meetings because they were invited as a "guest" to one specific meeting, noted in the minutes, and then automatically included on every subsequent circulation list. Check with people in advance about whether they consider their attendance to be absolutely necessary before sending out invitations. People often feel obliged to attend meetings because they are invited, not because they really want to or feel they should be there. More often than not, they would be just as happy receiving a brief summary of the discussion.

■ Whenever possible, aim to limit the size of the meeting to no more than seven people. The larger the group, the less time efficient the meeting becomes. Increased size also has the effect of reducing commitment.

■ An effective chairperson is critical—one who is sufficiently assertive to interrupt "wafflers" and allocate time limits on discussion. Directing discussion through the chair may be rather formal, but it curtails interruptions and affords everyone the opportunity to have a say. If the "official" chair is ineffective and starts to lose control, someone else needs to unofficially and tactfully take up the role.

■ Record actioned minutes with the name or initials of the person required to take action alongside. This ensures that everyone receives clear and specific instructions as to what he or she is required to do.

■ Use brainstorming techniques to generate ideas either within the meeting time or by asking individuals to brainstorm their ideas, but not censor them, in advance of the meeting.

■ Make notes on flip charts or whiteboards of points that the meeting may need to come back to later; this way, good suggestions will not be lost as discussion continues.

■ Suspend all telephone calls and ban portable telephones from any meeting.

■ Regularly change the seating arrangements and the meeting place to break up "cliques" and to avoid "set" patterns of interaction and thinking. Most people, given the choice, are likely to take up a position opposite their boss and next to a close colleague.

■ Remember, meetings are about listening as well as talking. To win a hearing at a meeting, it is important to listen actively to what others say. When making your point, demonstrate that you have heard what has been said by acknowledging what has gone before and that you understand its importance to the speaker(s); then raise your issue. Avoid jumping in and putting other people down; try to build on their ideas. Convince others of your point by focusing on the facts and issues rather than attacking personalities. Otherwise, they are likely to retaliate by personally attacking you, and the situation will escalate into conflict.

MAKING PRESENTATIONS

> *"It's not just a matter of life and death; it's much more important*
> *than that!"*

>   —Attributed to former Liverpool football club man-
>   ager, Bill Shankley, prior to an important game

If there is any single event in organizational life guaranteed to make
most managers break out into a cold sweat, it is the prospect of
having to make a presentation. Managerial jobs place a high emphasis on verbal communication skills, so managers are frequently asked
to present findings or make a case orally to their board or colleagues,
to speak to the press, or address various interest groups outside the
organization. Furthermore, the ability to deliver a good oral presentation is increasingly becoming an accepted and important feature of
many selection and assessment procedures within large organizations.

Presentations have several advantages over written reports:

- They are more personal and more imperative.
- They are less easily ignored.
- Any misunderstandings are more immediately evident and can be
  re-explained or expanded on.
- Feedback is more immediate.

Unfortunately, however, a bad presentation is better remembered
than a badly written report.

Generally, people are fearful of giving presentations. Performing in
public is an area of human activity for which most people traditionally
receive little or no formal training. Throughout our school and university education, success is essentially evaluated on the ability to
pass written rather than oral examinations. Consequently, getting up
and speaking to large groups of people is perceived to be an alien and
potentially uncomfortable experience and one most of us often do our
utmost to avoid.

Most of the fear and stress associated with making a presentation
arise from the speculative "what if" scenarios that run through an

individual's mind: "What if nobody laughs at my jokes?" "What if I dry up!" "What if somebody asks me a question I can't answer?" In the same way that actors talk of "dying" on stage, the aspiring manager dreads that a bad presentation may amount to career suicide.

Reducing the Area of the Unknown

Anybody who regularly watches television programs such as *News at Ten* will be familiar with the standardized format that it follows each evening. The program begins with a series of brief headlines that alert the viewer to the issues or news that are to be discussed. These issues are then addressed in more detail. Finally, the program closes with a further short review of the main points. Furthermore, the viewing audience knows in advance that the entire news presentation will be over within 30 minutes, which is ideal in terms of the length of the average viewer's concentration span. The format of *News at 10* illustrates what is recognized to be the three fundamental structural principles of any presentation:

1. Tell them what you are going to say (the opening or exposition).
2. Tell them (the main body—the development of ideas).
3. Then tell them again (the closing recapitulation).

The key to any good presentation is preparation. The more that one can reduce the area of the unknown, the more confident and in control the presenter will feel. Many of the things that go wrong with presentations and throw the presenter off balance—for example, arriving at the venue expecting an audience of around a dozen only to find an expectant audience sitting there of close to 100—can be avoided with some basic research and advanced planning. Preparation begins with five important questions.

1. *Why* are you giving this presentation? Is it to give information, obtain a consensus, initiate a course of action, or entertain? At the end of the presentation, what do you hope to have achieved?
2. *To whom* is it addressed? Who will be in the audience? How much do they know about the subject? What do they expect to learn? What

questions or objections are they likely to raise? Approximately how many will be there?

3. *Where* will the presentation take place? What will the layout of the room be like? What audiovisual equipment will be available? What do you need? Will a microphone be necessary?

4. *What* are you going to say? Make a list of all your points.

5. *How* will you make the presentation? And how long will you be expected to talk?

The What and the How. Before making a presentation, you have to plan carefully what you are going to say and then rehearse and time it. First impressions are very important, so every presentation needs a good opening to build the confidence of both the speaker and members of the audience so that they can sit back and relax, reassured that they are in capable hands. A good opening does not necessarily have to include a joke, although it can help. If you are not confident that you are a good or a natural joke teller, avoid jokes altogether— when they go flat, they can be extremely embarrassing.

However, before you even start, check first that everybody can hear you and will be able to see any overheads or slides you may use. Having to repeat oneself in a louder voice after a false start can seriously undermine confidence. Begin with a few welcoming courtesies; introduce yourself and state what you are going to present. It is important to outline your route map. Remember that your audience does not know what you are going to say. This means, fortunately, that they won't know what you miss or might forget to say. However, people listen better when they are prepared for what's coming next. To avoid the possibility of their switching off in the first few minutes, give them a few signposts by briefly explaining the structure of your presentation, including how long it will last and when they can ask questions. Most presenters feel more comfortable handling questions at the end rather than dealing with them as they go along. This allows them more control over the proceedings. They are also less likely to become sidetracked and lose concentration if the flow of the presentation is uninterrupted. Also, the odds are that many early queries are likely to be automatically covered during the course of the presentation.

It has been suggested that most business presentations can be structured using a 6P plan:

Preface (introduction)
Position (current situation)
Problem (what it is)
Possibilities (alternatives)
Proposal (suggested or recommended solution)
Postscript (outcome/presentation objectives)

As you move from one part of the presentation to the next, you will need to introduce a paragraph to enable the audience to make the connection. Otherwise, you may lose them. Psychological research has shown that people remember material better when it is presented to them in categories or headings. In presentations, these "labels" have to be given verbally and/or presented on overheads or slides.

In 1972, Bransford and Johnson conducted an interesting psychological experiment that illustrates the importance of triggers such as headings in "switching on" attention and aiding memory recall. They presented subjects with the following information and then asked them what it was about.

> The procedure is actually quite simple. First, you arrange items into different groups. Of course, one pile may be sufficient depending on how much there is to do. If you have to go somewhere else due to lack of facilities, that is the next step; otherwise, you are pretty well set. It is important not to overdo things. In the short run this may not seem important but complications can easily arise. A mistake can be expensive as well. At first the whole procedure will seem complicated. Soon, however, it will become just another facet of life. It is difficult to foresee any end to the necessity for this task in the immediate future, but then one can never tell. After the procedure is complete, one arranges the materials into their appropriate places. Eventually, they will be used once more and the whole cycle will then have to be repeated. However, that is part of life.

Until they gave the subjects the simple heading "Washing Clothes," the piece was virtually unintelligible; many people had "switched off" after the first couple of sentences.

Finally, close with a brief summary, offer a word of thanks, take a deep breath, and invite your audience to ask questions.

Some Helpful Hints on Content and Style

■ Avoid jargon and acronyms. They may be unfamiliar to your audience, even if they are members of your own organization.

■ Have some form of memory aid. Numbered notecards with your key points on them are excellent. They can be easily and unobtrusively held in your hand. It is a good idea to note on these cards the point at which you wish to introduce a slide or overhead and to write in cues for yourself, such as "smile" or "pause."

■ Pauses are important. When a person is nervous or excited, he or she tends to speak faster than normal; this is particularly true of females, who normally speak faster than males anyway. Deliberately taking time to pause helps slow down delivery, can help emphasize or punctuate what you say, and gives you a chance to take a deep breath.

■ If you are using autocue, you will need to prepare a script of exactly what you are going to say and adhere rigidly to it; otherwise the autocue operator will become confused—and subsequently, so will you!

■ Remember when you are preparing the presentation that written language can sound strange when spoken. Use short, punchy sentences and words you would use in normal conversation.

■ If you are quoting statistics rather than giving exact numbers, which are hard and take time for the memory to process (e.g., 1,627), round them up or down and quote approximations (e.g., approximately 1,600).

■ Try to include hypothetical examples or analogies to illustrate what you are saying.

■ Remember the concentration of span of your listeners. In any listening situation, there is always a strong primacy-recency effect. The listener is more likely to recall what you said first and what you said last and probably only about 50% of what you said in the middle. Ideally, presentations should be no more than 45 minutes, including questions.

■ If your presentation is intended to be persuasive and result in a commitment that involves financial expenditure, sell your idea first—then present the costs at the end.

Visual Aids

Any presentation is usually more effective if it appeals to more than one sense in terms of interest and reinforcement of the verbal message.

Typically, this is achieved by visual aids (i.e., overhead transparencies, slides, or handouts). However, if it is appropriate to the presentation, passing around work samples (e.g., machine parts) to illustrate what you are talking about can be extremely effective in that they appeal to two senses simultaneously (i.e., sight and touch).

When preparing visual aids, it is important not to include too much; three or four brief points in large typeset are sufficient. Detailed financial information or complex flow charts are better presented in the form of individual handouts that people can study while you talk. Be careful if you experiment with color; color transparencies may look pretty, but some colors (for example, blue) are extremely difficult to read at a distance. It is good practice to use a pointer to avoid a common mistake made by many presenters of standing silhouetted by the screen and masking the actual transparencies. Arrange your slides or transparencies in order before you start. Try not to include too many; their purpose is to aid your presentation, not turn it into a picture show (a video would do the job much better!). About five or six transparencies are generally sufficient for an average-length presentation.

A whiteboard or flip chart can be good for impromptu illustrations, but lengthy use interrupts the flow because your back is to the audience. Slides tend to be more expensive than overhead transparencies. Also, their ordering is particularly crucial because they have the disadvantage of overhead transparencies in that it is more difficult to flip back or flip ahead, if you need to refer back to something or you are running out of time. Asking a colleague to take responsibility for operating the slide projector can relieve stress and leave you free to concentrate on what you are saying, provided that he or she is adequately rehearsed. Sometimes, the siting of the speaker's platform in relation to the projection equipment necessitates the use of an "extra hand."

Some Basic Dos

■ Rehearse: Ideally, rehearse in front of others and ask for feedback. Alternatively, practice in front of the mirror or videotape or record yourself. Critically listen to yourself; remove and replace words that you find yourself stumbling over. Watch out for the overuse of catch phrases, such as "if you know what I mean," and annoying physical mannerisms, fidgeting, and so on. If you are involved in a group presentation, practice as a group; familiarize yourself with what others are going to say to avoid overlap and to ensure that if a member suddenly gets sick or is delayed in traffic, you can act as understudy.

■ Never read verbatim from notes or try to memorize the whole presentation. If you are reading, you cannot maintain eye contact. If you look up and are dependent on a verbatim script for what comes next, the chances are that when you look down, you will have lost your place and panic! As everybody who has ever taken an examination knows, memory can also be extremely unreliable under conditions of extreme stress.

■ The practice of placing a sheet of paper over an overhead transparency and gradually sliding it down to reveal each individual point, fortunately, is no longer fashionable. The benefits to be gained by doing this are generally overshadowed by the irritation it causes the audience.

■ Distribute any handouts at the end or as you go along, never in advance. If you do this, people will read the handout rather than listen to you. You may also be inadvertently setting yourself up for some tricky questions at the end.

■ Remember, eye contact is important. If you panic, find a friendly face in the audience and fix on it. Smiling from time to time is also important.

■ Finally, seek the honest feedback of someone you know in the audience so that you can learn from the experience and improve next time.

Handling Questions

The key to handling questions well is to not get defensive and possibly end up arguing with the questioner. It is a good idea to ask from the outset for questioners to identify themselves prior to asking their questions. This will give you a handle on what their interests or motives are in raising the question so that you can appropriately tailor your answer. In a large audience, it is also appropriate to ask questioners to stand up to deliver their questions so that you can hear them clearly. If you don't fully hear a question, do not attempt to answer the bits you have heard and guess at the rest, ask for the question to be repeated.

Repeating the question is a tactic used by many experienced presenters, particularly politicians. It has a twofold purpose. It ensures that the rest of the audience hears the question clearly, and it gives you a few seconds breathing space to work on your answer. If you don't know the answer to a question, don't bluff; the questioner may be smarter than you, and your bluffing might expose that fact. The way around such a question is first to try to make the questioner feel good— You have raised an interesting and complex question." It must be or you would have already thought of it, so acknowledge it. Then either throw the question open to the floor or acknowledge that it is something you haven't thought of in any depth but would like to discuss in some detail with the questioner, perhaps after the presentation.

Managing Stress

We have discussed in some detail ways and techniques for preparing and delivering effective presentations. In this section, we provide a few final tips for calming prepresentation nerves:

- Arrive ahead of time so you can check out the room one final time and compose yourself.
- Avoid eating or drinking in the hour before, for obvious reasons. When under stress, digestion slows down and the urge to urinate increases and can make for an uncomfortable presentation. Many actors suck on a piece of hard candy before a performance to moisten the mouth and combat dryness. (Black currant lozenges are reported to be particularly effective.)
- Check yourself out in a mirror before you go on. The unzipped fly (or in the case of females, the ladder in the stocking) may be a music hall joke, but you don't want it happening to you.
- Practice deep breathing and a few relaxation exercises to release tension.
- Voice delivery and projection are better if you stand up to present.
- Have water with no ice (you may inadvertently choke on it) at your side, and when you pause, take a sip to keep your mouth moist.
- Practice, practice, practice . . .

Talking to the Press

Working as a senior manager in either the public or private sector nowadays means dealing with the press. Environmental concerns, downsizing, mergers and acquisitions, and joint ventures are only a few of the issues that increasingly force contact between managers and the media. The skills of dealing appropriately with the media, whether newspapers, TV, or radio, are not usually found in MBA courses or indeed in generic management training courses. For managers to reduce the hassles or stress associated with press coverage of corporate events, it is important to remember some simple rules:

- Prior to a press conference or media interview, write down the two or three points you would like conveyed.

- Remember, for press and media interviewers "bad news is good news," so be careful and stick to your planned points—don't deviate.

- Don't appear defensive; keep your points short and wait for the next question. Try not to fill in silences. Wait to be asked the next question rather than rambling on; otherwise, you might say something you will later regret.

- If you don't have an immediate answer, indicate that you "will get back to [him or her] on that point," asking the interviewer to call you later that day or tomorrow.

- If you are called up and asked for an immediate response to some important corporate problem, don't respond until you have thought through the implications of your alternative responses. Ask to be called back later in the day.

- If you can turn a negative event into a positive one, highlighting some future action in the same or an allied area, do so. On the other hand, if the event or incident is patently your organization's fault and if legal advice permits, own up to the responsibility and describe future action to rectify or prevent such events from occurring again.

Organizations should be cognizant of the importance of external communications, not only in terms of their image but also in minimizing the potential stress for the manager confronted by the media. Regular courses on interviewing skills should be conducted so that managers are better able to deal with these events as and when they occur.

NOTE

1. From the 1989 Department of Transport Annual Statistics.

HOME AND WORK

Many of the hassles that people experience in contemporary life stem from the interface between work and home, primarily from the increase in dual-career families and how this affects roles and relationships at home. In fact, the junior Minister for Social Security, Alistair Burt, MP, in June 1993, indicated as much in a speech about work and the family: "Too many companies and businesses demand outrageous time commitments from those who work for them, without thought of the damage to family structure or for the strength their employees should get from a sound family life if they are allowed to foster it." This chapter will explore the changing nature of the family, the difficulties this causes, and how individuals might begin to deal with them.

THE CHANGING NATURE OF THE FAMILY

An interesting way of conceptualizing contemporary marriage has been provided by Charles Handy (1978). He studied husbands and wives in terms of their needs for achievement, dominance, affiliation,

and nurturance. As can be seen in Figure 6.1, he combined achievement and dominance needs and affiliation and nurturance needs to
come up with four patterns that reflect fundamental approaches to
life. To arrive at particular *marriage patterns,* he combined the husbands' orientations with those of the wives. Although there are 16
possible combinations of marriage patterns, Handy's research
turned up only 8, with 4 principal patterns occurring. We will look
at his 4 most frequent ones, as shown in Figure 6.1.

The first pattern was of a thrusting husband and a caring wife,
which Handy found to be the most frequent pattern and the one that
represents the traditional sex role stereotype. Here, the husband is the
breadwinner and the wife the homemaker. His goals of success and
achievement are her goals as well, and all her efforts are involved in
the home and providing him with support, although she is not particularly interested in the details of his work. These marriages are
predictable, structured, and create little stress.

The negative aspects of this pattern are that the wife has difficulty
in expressing or meeting her own needs while her children are around.
She also may find it difficult to cope when the children leave home or
the husband's career reaches its ceiling or, indeed, deteriorates.

The second marriage pattern is the pairing of two thrusters. In
this pattern, both the husband and the wife have high needs for
achievement and dominance. In the past, the thrusting wife tended
to stay at home and either be frustrated at not achieving her own goals
or attempt to meet her achievement need in homemaking activities. Thrusters usually desire support or the "caring" role, and if both
are making this demand known, considerable discontent can result.
This is also the pairing situation most likely to lead to dual-career
families, confronting the changing conception of a woman's role in
the home. Naturally, if both thrusters become thoroughly involved in
their work lives, as they are likely to do, their domestic arrangements
and circumstances are likely to be very chaotic indeed. Because, by
definition, thrusters—whether husband or wife—need the comforts
of the home environment, the conflicts, tensions, and stress in the
family will be enormous. In addition, these types of relationships
become very much more strained when children arrive on the scene
because the husband attempts to get his wife to play out the traditional
sex role stereotype (that is, she must give up her job) and draws on
the guilt he knows his wife has buried just below the surface of her
emancipation.

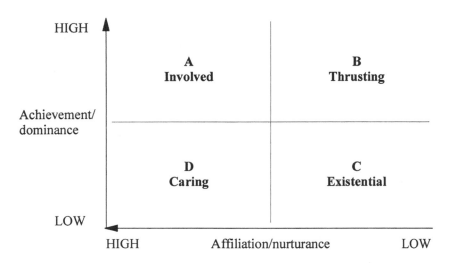

Figure 6.1. Types of Marriages
SOURCE: Handy (1978).

The third pattern is the partnership of two involved people. Although the husband and wife are both high achievers, with a tendency to be dominant in their interpersonal relationships, they also place a high value on caring and belonging. As Handy suggests, "They prefer to share arenas, not separate them." The stress level in these marriages is very high, because both partners have an underlying thrusting instinct, but this is tempered with a caring element that encourages them to confront one another with problems. In contrast, two thrusters would avoid resolution by compromise and discussion and would seek victory through defeat. Although in this third pattern one partner or the other may have to do something in the short run that he or she would prefer not to, there is sufficient flexibility in the marriage to provide short-term support so that he or she can end up doing what either wants to do in the longer term.

The last marriage pattern is an involved husband with a caring wife. Here, the husband is highly achievement orientated but also values the caring aspect of relationships. The husband is likely to be under a great deal of stress, because not only is he ambitious, he also cares about other people and is very concerned not to hurt others. Because the husband is sensitive to other people's feelings, he feels guilty when his wife commits herself solely to him (although he does want her social support). As Handy suggests, these relationships are "less predictable and the tensions less well contained. These relationships are more intense and emotional. There is more questioning and more effort to rework roles than in the traditional marriages."

Different combinations of roles can create problems, as Handy indicates:

1. If the activity pattern of a marriage fits that which would normally be required by the underlying mix of personalities, there will be less "familial stress." For example, if an A-A couple [see Figure 6.1] were forced by the success of the husband and the needs of the children to adopt a B-D pattern, family stress is likely to be increased.

2. If the pattern of husband-wife relationship doesn't change with changes in the central life interests of each member, there is liable to be more family stress.

3. If there are changes in the activity pattern at home or work which do not fit with one of the satisfactory marriage patterns above, then either the job or the attitudes of the partners must change if stress and conflict are to be avoided.

DEALING WITH DUAL-CAREER RELATIONSHIPS

Economic pressures and the needs of women to pursue careers outside the home have led Britain and many other Western countries into becoming dual-career cultures (Cooper, Cooper, & Eaker, 1988). Francine and Tim Hall (1980) suggest that the "traditional family model of the husband as breadwinner and wife as homemaker, together 'till death do us part,' is becoming a vestige of a past society." In the United States, less than 10% of American families are made up of the traditional working husband, homemaker wife, and two children, and in the United Kingdom, although the male labor force has increased by 3% in the past 20 years, the female labor force has grown by more than 40%.

Although the dual-career couple can be liberating, it can also create an enormous number of daily hassles for its participants. Like Handy, the Halls contend that the problems associated with two-career families can be great, depending on the nature of the marriage itself. They define the two-career couple as "two people who share a lifestyle that includes (1) cohabitation, (2) separate work roles for both partners, and (3) a love relationship that supports and facilitates both. "They contend that there are four dual-career family role structures: accommodators, adversaries, allies, and acrobats. The *accommodator* pattern usually has "one partner who is high in career involvement and low in home involvement, while the other partner is high in home involvement and low in career involvement." The difference between this pattern and the traditional family one is that either gender can play either role. The possible stresses and strains are kept to a minimum. There are an increasing number of men prepared to play the traditional female role while wives become the breadwinners—although the movement in this direction is insignificant in comparison to the number of families with working husbands and wives.

On the other hand, the *adversaries* are very much the two working thrusters described by Handy, a couple in which "both partners are highly involved in their careers, and have low involvement in home, family, or partner support roles" (Hall & Hall, 1980). As in the two-thruster marriages, this is the most stressful marital pattern, in which there is competition over priorities, avoidance of nonwork roles in the family, conflict in terms of career development of either member, and the unwillingness to give up any career identity to meet the needs of husband or wife or of the family unit (unless the work costs are negligible).

The third type is the *allies* pattern in which "two people are both highly involved in either career or home and family roles, with little identity tied up in the other." This is broken down into two different orientations. In the former, neither partner identifies with a career. Both derive their primary satisfaction from their family and their relationship. In the other, they identify strongly with their jobs and not the family, and "their identities are not tied up in having a well-ordered home, gourmet dinners, entertaining, or often, children. The support structure may be 'purchased,' in dinners out, maids, and catering services, or simply not exist." The potential stress problem in the latter case is that the couple doesn't have the time required to maintain the relationship as a support base for their independent activities.

The fourth type of couple is the *acrobats*. As the name implies this type of couple is made up of "partners who are highly involved in all their roles, both work and family." They perceive the home and work roles as equally important and, therefore, are very vulnerable to overload. As Hall and Hall suggest, their major source of stress derives from the "conflict of trying to meet all the demands—having a successful career, being a good partner, having a well-ordered home, providing real and emotional support for the spouse, and still finding time for the relationship."

Coping With Multiple Roles

Throughout the 1990s, the number of dual-career couples continues to grow, but society's expectations concerning family roles still tend to lag behind reality (Lewis & Cooper, 1989). If the activities of dual-career husbands and wives conflict with these expectations, this can cause conflict and guilt. Mothers of young children are particularly vulnerable to feelings of guilt, because they do not conform to society's traditional definition of a "good mother." Equally, some men feel that their masculinity is threatened if their powerful position as major breadwinner is challenged. Such problems are less severe for the "new man," but many individuals who articulate nontraditional views of these changing roles have difficulty in completely overcoming the powerful influence of their early socialization. This ambivalence about gender roles underlies problems such as "who does what in the home," where the family should locate, and commitments to child care.

The male work ethic, which fails to acknowledge the interdependence of work and family, issues of equality, and ambivalence about sex roles, complicates the lives of dual-career families. It cannot be denied that a dual-career way of life is very demanding and can be stressful at times, but it is also potentially satisfying and fulfilling.

Most of the research investigating coping strategies of dual-career couples has been based on a model developed by Tim Hall (1977). He describes three approaches to coping with multiple roles, as summarized by Sue Lewis and Cary Cooper (1989):

Type 1 Coping: Structure Role Redefinition. This is an attempt to alter other people's expectations of a particular role. For instance, a wife may renegotiate with her husband the expectation that she should be responsible for all domestic work, or an employee may negotiate with his or her boss about what should be expected in a particular job. Type 1 strategies include delegation and refusing to take on extra work.

Type 2 Coping: Personal Role Definition. This is an attempt by an individual to change his or her own self-expectations and behaviors, without necessarily trying to alter other people's attitudes. Making a personal decision to limit activities in the career, spousal, or parental roles would be examples of Type 2 coping. Strategies include eliminating roles—for example, giving up voluntary work or union activity, restricting social contacts, and establishing priorities.

Type 3 Coping: Reactive Role Behavior or Role Expansion. Instead of attempting to change the situation or alter self-expectations, an individual may attempt to organize himself or herself in such a way that all role demands can be met. For instance, an overworked mother may work even harder to fit the superwoman image rather than delegate more domestic work to her husband, reduce work involvement, or lower standards in the home. Strategies that enable individuals to do all this include planning, scheduling, working harder, and denying that a situation is stressful.

Coping Types 1 and 2 are both active coping orientations, in that they involve redefining roles in an attempt to make the situation more manageable. Type 3 coping or role expansion is more passive. It involves an acceptance of all role demands. Attempts are made to satisfy everyone's expectations by being more organized or by using techniques that will minimize the subsequent stress, without eliminating or reducing its cause.

Because role and overload problems tend to be greater for women, it is not surprising that the majority of research into the effectiveness of these strategies has examined the coping behavior of employed mothers. As Lewis and Cooper (1989) highlight, there is evidence that role redefinition (Types 1 and 2) tends to be more stressful, producing higher levels of career satisfaction, and to be more successful than role expansion in reducing conflicts between work and home (Beutell & Greenhaus, 1983). Nevertheless, different approaches, they suggest, tend to be used in relation to different situations. Active role redefinition strategies are perceived as more effective in dealing with work-related problems (Alpert & Culbertson, 1987), but mothers are generally reluctant to redefine expectations concerning the parental role. In addition, women who have traditional attitudes are more likely to try to fit everything in than are nontraditional women, who are better able to consider ways of adapting their role. Furthermore, although role redefinition strategies appear to be more effective overall, there is some evidence that they are less effective for professional women with young children because of internal guilt feelings (Gilbert, Holohan, & Manning, 1981). Underlying traditional attitudes toward motherhood make it very difficult, even for women who articulate nontraditional beliefs, to alter their own or other people's expectations of the role of good mother. Therefore, active coping strategies that aim to change people's expectations associated with specific roles are most effective, but women's early childhood experiences often prevent these techniques from being successful, because traditional attitudes to the maternal role elicit feelings of guilt.

Reducing the Working Family Tensions

In addition to dealing with the role problem in dual-career relationships, couples need to find specific techniques in reducing the tension to more adequately consider the deeper-level issues. Bebe Campbell-Moore (1988) suggests a series of steps in lowering the temperature when inevitable conflicts occur:

1. Find time to talk in a relaxed way. This may involve deliberately setting aside some time from busy schedules when lack of interruptions is guaranteed.
2. Learn techniques of effective communication. Using the wrong words can alienate. It is better to take responsibility for your own feelings and behavior than to accuse. For example, "I feel you could do more in the house" rather than "You never do enough in the house." Your feelings can be discussed, but an accusation merely makes the other person defensive.
3. Listen to what the other person says. It is useful to reflect back, to show that you have really heard and accept his or her feelings. For example, "It sounds as though you feel really angry with me. Can you tell me what I do that makes you feel that way?"

If problems have become really overwhelming—

4. It might help to agree to an official time out or call a temporary truce. A temporary separation, such as separate holidays, may provide time to work out a solution.

5. Don't try to solve all problems at once. Work on one at a time.

6. If necessary, elicit the help of a professional counselor.

Murray Watts and Cary Cooper (1992) also offer several suggestions for dealing with marital problems when one partner or both partners are showing signs of stress:

- People under severe stress lose their perspective. Try to keep yours.

- Don't let another's stress infect you, making you anxious. The problems will get much worse if you add to them. Use mental and physical relaxation exercises. Find space and time to be alone.

- Don't get drawn into endless rows. Your anger will serve to justify your partner's anger, which needs to be exposed as a problem.

- Be kind to yourself. Don't be a martyr. The carer needs caring for too. Make sure you have at least one person you can off-load your problems onto. Express your anger and frustrations to that person. Clear the air regularly.

- Look for "early warning" signs of stress in those you love. Choose a moment when your partner or relative is calm and relaxed. Gently point out your concern to him or her without any accusation: "I'm worried about you. You're smoking a lot more than you used to. You must feel under a lot of strain."

- Take action on the other's behalf in cases where his or her will is paralyzed: "I think we should talk about your depression to our doctor. Let me make an appointment. I'll come with you."

- When resistance to any change is put up over a long period, be firm. You cannot go on listening to the same gripes and moans thousands of times without your relationship's deteriorating. Be loving, but make it clear that you are not only a son, daughter, or wife but a person in your own right with your own needs. You need for the other person to find a way through.

- Be a "sounding board" but not a "duck board." If your feelings are being ignored and you are being trodden down, insist on some time away, a day or a weekend, with friends or alone. Keep renewing your strength.

- Don't be a "codependent," worsening the stressed person's problems by your need to care for him or her. Don't hold back the other's progress by indulging him or her because it makes you feel "needed."

The other person's self-destructive attitudes or behavior can never be the foundation for a healthy relationship.

- Be an "enabler." See yourself as the one who helps the sufferer to help herself or himself.

- Help the other person to focus on the present and the future, to talk about what can be done, not about what cannot be undone.

- Try making a list of problem areas in the other's life. Do it together. Look at some options.

- Believe for that person that things can change, without being unsympathetic or glib. Be your partner's eyes when he or she can't see beyond the problems at hand. Remind your partner that this is temporary. He or she will see clearly and hope again.

Managing Time Out

Another way in which couples can begin to cope with the pressures of everyday life is to create "time-out" periods in the year. It has been recently reported in the *Daily Express* that general practitioners are prescribing holiday brochures rather than pills for many of their hassled patients. In a survey, 83% of general practitioners believed that patients who took regular holidays had fewer stress problems, in spite of the fact that working people in Britain have fewer national holidays than their European counterparts: United Kingdom 33 days a year, compared to 41 for Germany, 36 for Italy, and 34 for France.

Managing time-out means creating time and space for you and your partner and, in some cases, for the children as well. Instead of people polluting the beaches of Spain or Portugal during the summer, perhaps dual-career couples ought to take frequent but short time-outs during the course of a stressful work year. There are a range of possible time-outs, each of which might serve a different function:

Time Out With Partner. When the signs are present that "things are not right" in the relationship (e.g., lack of any communication; constant avoidance activity, such as obsession with TV; increased irritability; etc.), it is time to get away together. Get someone to look after the kids, cats, plants, and the like and take a long weekend. Get away and allow yourselves some space and time to talk, to *be* with one another, to begin to open up.

Time Out With Family. The hassles of dual-career couples also adversely affect children, and occasionally it is necessary for whole families to take time out, whether on short holidays or long weekends away. The distress of children of working parents doesn't always manifest itself in an obvious way, but the symptoms are real and should be attended to, as this comment from an executive woman illustrates:

> My eldest boy is 14. He's such an uncommunicative character; communications happen but in grunts and sudden rushes of confidential information, and then silences that go on for days. He might suddenly show quite a warmth towards me when I come back from a business trip, which happens quite regularly. It seems to me to indicate that he has in some vague way been disturbed by my absence and is glad to see me back, even though he wouldn't like to say so.

Relocations

Another problematic home-work interface event is job relocations. The labor force in the United Kingdom and in Europe generally is becoming much more mobile, which is particularly the case for managers and other professionals. Indeed, it is now estimated that U.K. managers change jobs about once every 3 years. Research in North America and other Western countries suggests that managerial mobility there is increasing even more rapidly. But relocation, although more frequent among middle-class and white-collar workers, does not affect them alone. With the decline in the economy in the past couple of years and the increase in blue-collar unemployment, workers in the mining and steel industries have been encouraged to "pick up stakes" and leave their hometowns for greener pastures.

Whatever the background one comes from, moving can be a traumatic and stressful event, depending on two factors. The first involves the situation in which the individual is involved or his or her "life area," such as job, family, and outside activities. The second factor involves characteristics of the individual (age, qualifications, job skills, and personality)—that is, the base from which he or she views and interprets the world. These stresses are highlighted by the wife of a bank manager who has finally been forced to relocate:

What is often not realized by the bank is the tremendous burden that moving house places on the wife. Buying and selling houses is very time consuming, the average length of time for our moves being about 6 months. A promotion move occurs at any time; it may be a "difficult" time in the school year for children, the housing market may be awkward, the list is endless, but the bank takes very little account of any of the problems, and it is generally the wife who has the responsibility of sorting out the difficulties. The bank's attitude is that "wives like new carpets and curtains; therefore, they enjoy moving house!" This really annoys me—generalizing about women. Bank wives are not expected to "think," just to accept! We are supposed to conform to a set model—that of the perfect housewife, ready to comply to the demands of a husband's career; to enjoy homemaking but not to get so attached to our homes that we object to giving them up; to be totally dependent on our husbands, both financially and emotionally, yet capable of living apart for long periods; with the added ability of being a financial and legal organizer of the complexities and difficulties that surround buying and selling homes in two different parts of the country. The stereotyped role of the bank wife is full of contradictions.

It is not only the difficulties which surround the operation of buying and selling houses which bank wives have to cope with. The financial rewards of a promotion are negligible and often, for the first 12 months after a house move, people are financially worse off than before promotion. Also, a promotion carries exactly the same salary rise whether it involves a house move or not, so you don't even have the dubious consolation of a higher income to make up for all the disruptions and upsets to family life a house move can incur.

Cary Cooper and Judi Marshall (1979) carried out a study that explored the stresses and strains of job transfer on middle and senior executives in the United Kingdom. This study can help illustrate some of the problems for the individual relocating at different stages in life.

For instance, *younger single men* in the sample reported problems such as the pressure of starting a new job (at a critical and closely watched phase in their careers), the culture shock of starting work after life at a university, having no separate world to retire to in the evenings to help switch off, the problems of house hunting, being lonely in a strange town (often populated by "contented" married couples), leaving friends behind and trying to maintain contacts (perhaps with a possible future wife).

For *young marrieds*, it appeared that most couples felt free and willing to meet the challenge of a new community; it is typically at this time that they have most friends and activities outside the home. Their lack of constraints makes it easier to follow one or the other's career, to be more mobile. In a dual-career marriage, complications arise: Is one partner to sacrifice his or her career for the promotional move of the other? How does the partner find another rewarding occupation after the move? If both have busy careers, how do they manage the complexities of finding a new home and moving, and are they able, in their limited spare time, to form new social relationships?

For *married couples with a young family*, the problems of relocations are complex, both for the more traditional marriage, in which the wife is at home, and for the dual-career family. For the latter, house hunting becomes a major problem, both because the wife is too tied down to participate much and because house choice becomes more crucial and the criteria more exacting. Size and nearness to schools and shops become important, and for the housebound wife, potential friends must also be considered. Separation is an emotionally draining time for all of the family. If the wife is at home, her adaptation to and happiness in her new environment become critical factors. The couple may find it harder to make friends away from work, tied down as they are, and place more emphasis on "nearness" (the neighbors) *and* "same-boat" acquaintances (couples with children of the same age and interests). They must find new social support systems and new child and home help if they both work.

The children, as Ivancevich and Matteson (1980) suggest, are also affected by the move:

> Certain age groups are more susceptible to relocation stress. Pre-schoolers experience feelings of loss and insecurity. They may even interpret a relocation as a form of punishment. A young child may revert to infantile behaviour such as thumb-sucking and bed-wetting or they may experience more nightmares. Children in grade school may experience similar feelings of insecurity. Teen-agers, to whom peer approval and relationships are so important, frequently have a particularly difficult time.

Relocation is, therefore, an extremely stressful event at this stage.

Empty nesters, many of whom are still moving at this stage of life, may have come to regard mobility as an acceptable way of life. Others, however, express concern that they never settle down anywhere and that they are not providing a stable home for their children and grandchildren to visit. Choosing retirement sites becomes a problem for those who have lived in so many places and belonged to none.

Relocation is a recurring problem, often inducing stress for a number of family members. In the 1990s and beyond, with more women pursuing careers, the prospects for professional men or women being available for rapid deployment will substantially decrease. This will create a number of stressful choices for the partners in terms of the direction and the security of their careers.

Relocation: Exploring Possibilities and Alternatives. As Lewis and Cooper (1989) suggest, it is often necessary for married couples faced with the prospect of the relocation of one spouse to deviate from accepted norms of behavior. The "traditional pattern" is for the wife to move with her husband's job, whereas the husband's moving with his wife's job is unconventional. There are various strategies between these two extremes. Making your position clear from the outset may be one way of anticipating and avoiding future dilemmas. Lewis and Cooper suggest a range of positions that can be stated clearly after taking up employment:

1. Make it clear that you will not be willing to relocate.
2. Make it clear that you will not be willing to relocate unless a suitable position is also found for your spouse.
3. Make it clear from the outset that you are willing to relocate and that your family poses no obstacle. This may be particularly necessary for married women who may be passed over for promotion on the assumption that they cannot be mobile.
4. State that requests for relocation will be considered in the light of circumstances at the time, including your spouse's career situation, children's schooling, and so on.

At a later stage, dilemmas may still arise. If so, Lewis and Cooper feel that you should consider the following alternatives:

1. Refuse to relocate. This may involve loss of promotion and will reflect your life priorities.
2. If the new location is not too geographically distant, consider moving so that both of you can travel to work from one home that is approximately equidistant from your work locations. This may involve substantial traveling time.

3. Consider alternating decisions in each partner's favor. A move may be made now to facilitate one person's career on the understanding that the next move will favor the other spouse.
4. Consider living apart during the week or for longer periods.
5. Consider whether it is possible for one partner to work from home.
6. Consider other creative solutions. Mary Maples (1981) suggests that one solution may be for one partner to take up flying as a hobby!

If you are faced with a relocation dilemma, it may be useful to list these and any other strategies you can think of and write down what might be the advantages and disadvantages of each one. Any decision will involve some sacrifice, in terms of career prospects, family life, or traveling time. Your final decision will depend on where your priorities lie in terms of your life values.

How Organizations Can Help Working Parents

Until recently, few employers did much to help working women with children to juggle the demands of job and family. Some companies developed job-sharing and part-time work schemes. But many of these were limited to jobs of low status, with restricted access to training and few opportunities for promotion.

Now, however, as more companies realize the need to rethink their working arrangements for career couples, a number of alternatives are proving their worth, as Suzan Lewis and Cary Cooper suggest (1989).

V-Time. This stands for voluntary reduced time—a system that allows full-time employees to reduce working hours for a specified period with a reduction in salary. It differs from the usual concept of part-time work in that it is temporary, with a return to full-time work guaranteed.

All employee benefits are maintained, although they may be altered to a pro rata basis. Usually, the schedule remains in force for an agreed period, perhaps 6 or 12 months, to allow employees and employers to try it out, with an assurance that the commitment can be renegotiated or terminated.

The time off may be taken by working shorter days or weeks; or a block of time may be taken, perhaps during school holidays. The

Alliance & Leicester Building Society has introduced a pilot scheme that allows time off during the holidays for those with children between the ages of 5 and 14. V-time may also be used for gaining new skills or responding to a health problem.

Career-Break Schemes. Fewer than 7% of women in the United Kingdom return to full-time work immediately after maternity leave, but 90% return after a longer break. Some organizations, recognizing that many women prefer to spend more time with their infants than maternity leave allows, have taken steps to provide longer career breaks. Reentry and retainer schemes have been initiated (e.g., by NatWest Bank, Barclays, ICL) to allow employees to interrupt their usual work for a number of years, after which they can return with no loss of seniority. The employee is usually expected to undertake at least 2 weeks' paid relief work for the company during each year of her absence and is provided with regular information packs and a refresher course on her return. In practice, many work for more than 2 weeks a year.

The scheme may permit one 5-year break or two shorter breaks, each dating from the end of statutory maternity leave. Many women prefer the two breaks, which enables them to return to work between the births of a first and second child.

Career breaks are open, in principle, to men as well as women, although in practice they tend to be taken only by women. Organizations permitting two short breaks could encourage their being shared between the two parents.

The benefits of a career-break scheme are becoming increasingly apparent:

- They ensure that participants remain in touch with their work, maintaining confidence, expertise, and knowledge.
- Firms offering career breaks will attract young women with talent and ambition, because they will have less fear of having to choose between family and career.
- They ensure that investment in training is not lost and that after a break, a minimum of retraining is required.
- They provide role models of women successfully combining career and family.
- They improve motivation, time keeping, and productivity.

- They increase flexibility by providing a pool of trained staff to draw on when people are absent or during peak periods.
- They reduce stress for new mothers and fathers.

The career-break scheme first introduced by NatWest has served as a model for many forward-looking organizations and professional bodies that are now adopting similar schemes. The Law Society suggests that those operating such a scheme should ensure maximum benefit by advertising themselves as "a career-break employer," in much the same way as many organizations claim to be equal-opportunity employers.

Sabbaticals. In Sweden, the idea of up to a year off, after a certain period of work, has been institutionalized in a wide range of occupations. In the United Kingdom, 6-month sabbaticals for employees aged 50 or over, with at least 25 years' service, have been introduced by the John Lewis group to allow employees to do things they enjoy that would not otherwise be possible.

Sabbaticals are available at all levels. People in specialist and senior management posts are encouraged not to feel indispensable, although they are required to give longer notice than other employees. Arrangements are made to cover their absences by creating an opportunity for a trainee or reorganizing colleagues' responsibilities to share the work.

This provides opportunities for employees to take on new responsibilities, which can contribute to personal and career development. Colleagues are willing to cooperate, knowing that they, too, will have the opportunity of a sabbatical.

Clearly, the age requirement in this particular scheme rules it out for new parents, but sabbaticals may be used to fulfill other family obligations that occur at a later stage. Apart from the care of sick relatives, people might wish to spend the time visiting adult children living abroad, for example. But the fact that the system works well has implications for the organization granting a leave of absence for younger employees, especially for those taking maternity or paternity leave.

Men as well as women can benefit from policies that aim to ease the transition to parenthood. Just as women need role models who successfully combine career and motherhood, men need role models of fathers willing to accommodate their careers for child care. Organizations can play a part in bringing about a change in attitudes. They can encourage fathers who show an interest in paternity leave or career breaks by guaranteeing that their career prospects will not be harmed. Ultimately, the most helpful organizations will be those offering the most choices to new parents so that they can suit their needs.

The 1980s was the era of the entrepreneurial and thrusting organization; the 1990s is likely to be one of corporate and community responsibility for the family, as Alistair Burt, junior Minister of Social Security, suggests:

> The success of the 1980's in Conservative political terms was to re-state the role of the individual in society, and in that classic phrase 'roll back the frontiers of the state' in so many different ways. But whilst this was a success in economic terms, it left a gap in our thinking in the development of social policy. There is such a thing as society, and it stands or falls on the strength of the individuals who make it up. The 80's was all about empowering the individual, but what we have to do in the 1990's is seek to marry such empowerment with a community structure which makes use of it.

References

Adair, J. (1982). *Effective time management*. London: Pan Books.

Akersted, T. (1985). Shifted sleep hours. *Annals of Clinical Research, 27*(5), 273-279.

Albrecht, K. (1979). *Stress and the manager: Making it work for you*. Englewood Cliffs, NJ: Prentice Hall.

Alfred Marks Bureau. (1982). *Sex in the office*. London: Author.

Alpert, D., & Culbertson, A. (1987). Daily hassles and coping strategies of dual career and non-dual earner women. *Psychology of Women Quarterly, 11*, 359-366.

Altendorf, D. M. (1986). *When cultures clash: A case study of the Texaco takeover of Getty Oil and the impact of acculturation on the acquired firm*. Unpublished doctoral dissertation, Graduate School of Business Administration, University of Southern California.

Bart, P. B. (1981). A study of women who were raped and avoided rape. *Journal of Social Issues, 37*, 123-137.

Basowitz, H., Persky, H., Karchin, S. J., & Grinker, R. R. (1955). *Anxiety and stress*. Englewood Cliffs, NJ: Prentice Hall.

Beals, C., Hopson, B., & Scally, M. (1991). *Assertiveness: A positive process*. London: Mercury Business Paperbacks.

Berne, E. (1964). *Games people play*. New York: Grove.

Beutell, N. J., & Greenhaus, J. H. (1983). Integration of home and non-home roles: Women's conflict and coping behaviour. *Journal of Applied Psychology, 68*, 43-48.

Bradley, G. (1983). Effects of computerization on work environment and health from the perspective of equality between sexes. *Occupational Health Nursing, 31,* 35-39.

Bransford, J. & Johnson, M. (1973). Consideration of some problems and comprehension. In W. D. Chase (Ed.), *Visual and information processing.* New York: Academic Press.

Breslow, L., & Buell, P. (1960). Mortality from coronary heart disease and physical activity of work in California. *Journal of Chronic Diseases, 11,* 615-625.

Buck, V. (1972). *Working under pressure.* London: Staples.

Burke, T., Madock, S., & Rose, A. (1993). *How ethical is British business?* Research Working Paper Series 2, No. 1, University of Westminster, Faculty of Business, Management & Social Studies.

Campbell-Moore, B. (1988). *Successful women: Angry men.* London: Arrow.

Caplan, R. D., Cobb, S., French, J. R. P., Van Harrison, R., & Pineau, S. R. (1975). *Job demands and worker health: Main effects and occupational differences.* NIOSH Research Report, Cincinnati, OH.

Carruthers, M. E. (1976, April). *Risk factor control.* Paper presented to the conference on Stress of Air Traffic Control Officers, Manchester, UK.

Cartwright, S., & Cooper, C. L. (1989). Predicting success in joint venture organisations in information technology—A cultural perspective. *Journal of General Management, 15,* 39-52.

Cartwright, S., & Cooper, C. L. (1992). *Mergers and acquisitions: The human factor.* Oxford: Butterworth Heinemann.

Cartwright, S., Cooper, C. L., & Barron, A. (1993). Manager stress and road accidents. *Journal of General Management, 19*(2), 78-85.

Cascio, W. F. (1993). Downsizing: What do we know? What have we learned? *Academy of Management Executive, 7*(1), 95-104.

Chalykoff, J., & Kochan, T. A. (1989). Computer-aided monitoring: Its influence on employee job satisfaction and turnover. *Personnel Psychology, 42,* 807-834.

Cobb, S., & Rose, R. H. (1973). Hypertension, peptic ulcer and diabetes in air traffic controllers. *Journal of the Australian Medical Association, 224,* 489-492.

Coch, L., & French, J. R. P. (1948). Overcoming resistance to change. *Human Relations, 1,* 395-407.

Cohen, L. R. (1983). Nonverbal (mis)communication between managerial men and women. *Business Horizons, 26*(1), 13-17.

Colatosi, C., & Karg, E. (1992). *Stopping sexual harassment: A handbook for union and workplace activists.* Detroit, MI: Labor Education and Research Project.

Cooper, C. L. (1984). Executive stress: A ten country comparison. *Human Relations, 1,* 395-407.

Cooper, C. L. (1991, June 10). The meeting. *The Independent on Sunday,*

Cooper, C. L., Cooper, R. D., & Eaker, L. D. (1988). *Living with stress.* London: Penguin.

Cooper, C. L., & Lewis, S. (1994). *The workplace revolution: Managing today's dual career families.* London: Kogan Page.

Cooper, C. L., Liukkonen, P., & Cartwright, S. (1996). *Stress prevention in the workplace: Assessing the costs and benefits to organizations.* Luxembourg: European Foundation for the Improvement of Living and Working Conditions.

Cooper, C. L., Makin, P., & Cox, C. (1989). *Managing people at work.* London: Routledge (in association with the British Psychological Society).

Cooper, C. L., & Marshall, J. (1979). *Executives under pressure*. London: Macmillan.

Cooper, C. L., & Payne, R. (1988). *Causes, coping and consequences of stress at work*. Chichester, UK: Wiley.

Cooper, C. L., & Sadri, G. (1991). The impact of stress counseling at work. *Journal of Social Behaviour & Personality, 6*(7), 411-423.

Cooper, C. L., & Smith, M. J. (1985). *Job stress and blue collar work*. New York: John Wiley.

Cox, C., & Cooper, C. L. (1988). *High fliers: An anatomy of managerial success*. New York: Blackwell.

Cox, M., & Cox, C. (1980). Ten years of transactional analysis. In J. Beck & C. Cox (Eds.), *Advances in management education*. New York: John Wiley.

Cox, T. (1978). *Stress*. London: Macmillan.

Crull, P. (1982). Stress effects of sexual harassment on the job: Implications for counseling. *American Journal of Orthopsychiatry, 52,* 539-544.

Cummings, T., & Cooper, C. L. (1979). A cybernetic framework for the study of occupational stress. *Human Relations, 32,* 395-419.

Dale, B., & Cooper, C. L. (1992). *Total quality and human resources*. Oxford, UK: Blackwell.

Di Tecco, D., Cwitco, G., Arsenault, A., & Andre, M. (1992). Operator stress and monitoring practices. *Applied Ergonomics, 23*(1), 29-34.

Earnshaw, J., & Cooper, C. L. (1996). *Stress and employer liability*. London: IPD.

Eggert, M. (1991). *Outplacement: A guide to management and delivery*. London: Institute of Personnel Management.

Equal Opportunities Commission. (1983). *Sexual harassment of women at work: A study from West Yorkshire*. Manchester, UK: Author.

Equal Opportunities Working Party. (1981). *Report on sexual harassment*. Liverpool, UK: NALGO.

French, J. R. P., & Caplan, R. D. (1972). Organizational stress & individual strain. In A. J. Marrow (Ed.), *The failure of success* (pp. 31-66). New York: Amacom.

Froggatt, H., & Stamp, P. (1991). *Managing pressure at work*. London: BBC Books.

Gilbert, L. A., Holohan, C. K., & Manning, L. (1981). Coping with conflict between professional and maternal roles. *Family Relations,* 319-426.

Gross, R. D. (1987). *Psychology: The science of mind and behaviour*. London: Edward Arnold.

Gutek, B. A. (1985). *Sex and the workplace*. San Francisco: Jossey-Bass.

Hall, F. S., & Hall, T. (1980). *The two-career couple*. Reading, MA: Addison-Wesley.

Handy, C. (1978). The family: Help or hindrance. In C. L. Cooper & R. Payne (Eds.), *Stress at work* (pp. 107-123). London: Wiley.

Harris, T. A. (1969). *I'm okay—you're okay: A practical guide to transactional analysis*. New York: Harper & Row.

Harrison, R. (1972, May/June). Understanding your organization's character. *Harvard Business Review,* pp. 119-128.

Harrison, R. (1987). *Organisational culture and quality of service: A strategy for releasing love in the workplace*. London: Association for Management Education and Development.

Heller, J. (1975). *Something happened*. New York: Ballantine.

Herriot, P. (1995). Psychological contracts. In N. Nicholson (Ed.), *Encyclopaedic dictionary of organizational behaviour*. Oxford, UK: Basil Blackwell.

Hinkle, L. E. (1973). The concept of stress in the biological social sciences. *Stress Medicine and Man, 1,* 31-48.

Holmes, T., & Cartwright, S. (1993). Career change post 35: Myth or reality. *Employee Relations, 15*(6), 37-54.

Holmes, T. H., & Rahe, R. H. (1967). The social readjustment rating scale. *Journal of Psychosomatic Research, 11,* 213-218.

Hopson, B., & Scally, M. (1993). *Build your own rainbow.* San Diego, CA: Pfieffer.

Ivancevich, J. M., & Matteson, M. T. (1980). *Stress at work.* Glenview, IL: Scott, Foresman.

Ivancevich, J. M., Matteson, M. T., & Richards, E. P. (1985, March-April). Who's liable for stress at work. *Harvard Business Review.*

Ivancevich, J. M., Schweiger, D. M., & Power, F. R. (1987). Strategies for managing human resource issues during mergers and acquisitions. *Human Resource Planning, 12*(1), 19-35.

Jensen, I. W., & Gutek, B. A. (1983). Attributions and assignment of responsibility in sexual harassment. *Journal of Social Issues, 38*(4), 121-136.

Johannson, G., & Aronsson, G. (1984). Stress reactions in computerized administrative work. *Journal of Occupational Behaviour, 5,* 159-181.

Karasek, R., & Theorell, T. (1990). *Healthy work: Stress, productivity and the reconstruction of working life.* New York: John Wiley.

Lazarus, R. S. (1966). *Psychological stress & coping process.* New York: McGraw-Hill.

Lazarus, R. S. (1976). *Patterns of adjustment.* New York: McGraw-Hill.

Levinson, H. (1973). Problems that worry our executives. In A. J. Marrow (Ed.), *The failure of success.* New York: AMACOM.

Lewis, S., & Cooper, C. L. (1989). *Career couples.* London: Unwin Hyman.

Liff, S. (1990). Clerical workers and information technology: Gender relations and occupational change. *New Technology, Work and Employment, 5*(1), 44-55.

Lunde-Jensen, P. (1994). The costs of occupational accidents and work related sickness in the Nordic countries. *Janus, 18*(4), 25-26.

Makin, P., Cooper, C. L., & Cox, C. (1988). *Managing people at work.* London: Routledge.

Maples, M. (1981). Dual career marriages: Elements for potential success. *Personnel & Guidance Journal, September,* 19-23.

Margolis, B., Kroes, W., & Quinn, R. (1974). Job stress: An unlisted occupational hazard. *Journal of Occupational Medicine, 16*(10), 654-661.

McClelland, D.C. (1961). *The achieving society.* Princeton, NJ: Van Nostrand.

Medea, A., & Thompson, K. (1974). *Against rape.* New York: Farrar, Strauss & Giroux.

Melhuish, A. (1978). *Executive health.* London: Business Books.

Mirvis, P. H. (1985). Negotiations after the sale: The roots and ramifications of conflict in an acquisition. *Journal of Occupational Behaviour, 6*(1), 65-84.

Murphy, L. R., Hurrell, J. J., Jr., Sauter, S. L., & Keita, G. P. (Eds.). (1995). *Job stress interventions.* Washington, DC: American Psychological Association.

Nelson, S., Cooper, C. L. & Jackson, P. R. (1993). Uncertainty amidst change: The impact of privatisation on employee job satisfaction and well-being. *Journal of Occupational and Organizational Psychology, 68*(1), 57-73.

Nelson-Bolles, R. (1995). *What color is your parachute?* Berkeley, CA: Ten Speed Press.

Nielsen, R. (1987). What can managers do about unethical management? *Journal of Business Ethics, 6*(4), 309-320.

Nussbaum, K., & du Rivage, V. (1989). Computer monitoring: Mismanagement by remote control. *Business & Society Review, 56*, 16-20.

Oldham, G. R. (1985). Effects of changes in work space partitions and spatial density of employee reactions: A quasi experiment. *Journal of Applied Psychology, 73*, 253-258.

Phillips, C. M., Stockdale, J. E., & Joeman, L. M. (1989). *The risks in going to work, the nature of people's work, the risks they encounter and the incidence of sexual harassment, physical attack and threatening behaviour.* London: Suzy Lamplugh Trust.

Pincherle, A. (1972). Fitness for work. *Proceedings of the Royal Society of Medicine, 65*, 321-324.

Pitturro, M. C. (1989). Employee performance monitoring . . . or meddling? *Management Review, 78*, 31-33.

Popovich, P. M., & Licata, B. J. (1987). A role model approach to sexual harassment. *Journal of Management, 13*(1), 149-161.

Quick, J. C., & Quick, J. D. (1984). *Organizational stress and preventive management.* New York: McGraw-Hill.

Robinson, S. L., & Morrison, E. W. (1995). Psychological contracts and organization citizenship behaviour: The effect of unfulfilled obligations on civic virtue behaviour. *Journal of Organizational Behaviour, 16*, 289-298.

Rousseau, D. M. (1990). New hire perceptions of their own and their employer's obligations: A study of psychological contracts. *Journal of Organizational Behaviour, 11*, 389-400.

Rubenstein, M. (1988). *The dignity of women at work.* Luxembourg: Commission of the European Communities.

Rubin, Z., & McNeil, E. B. (1983). *The psychology of being human* (3rd ed.). London: Harper & Row.

Russek, H. I., & Zohman, B. L. (1958). Relative significance of heredity, diet and occupational stress in CHD of young adults. *American Journal of Medical Sciences, 235*, 266-275.

Sauter, J. T., Hurrell, S., & Cooper, C. L. (1989). *Job control and worker health.* New York: John Wiley.

Schweiger, D. M., Ivancevich, J. M., & Power, F. R. (1987). Executive actions for managing human resources before and after acquisitions. *Academy of Management Executive, 2*, 127-138.

Searby, F. (1969, September-October). Control of post merger change. *Harvard Business Review,*

Selye, H. (1946). The general adaptation syndrome and the diseases of adaptation. *Journal of Clinical Endocrinology, 6*, 117.

Social Trends. (1990). Central Statistical Office, London: HMSO.

Sparrow, P. R. (1995). *The changing nature of psychological contracts in the UK banking sector: Does it matter?* Working Paper, 95-135, Sheffield University Management School.

Spindler, S. G. (1994). Psychological contracts in the workplace—A lawyer's view. *Human Resource Management, 33*(3), 325-334.

Studner, P. (1989). *Super job search.* London: Mercury.

Super, D. (1957). *The psychology of careers.* New York: Harper & Row.

Torrington, D., & Cooper, C. L. (1990, December 9). How to create a new life after 50. *Sunday Times.*

Townend, A. (1991). *Developing assertiveness*. London: Routledge.

UGT (General Union of Workers). (1987). *Investigacion sobre discriminacion y acaso sexual femenino en el puesto de trabajo*. Madrid: Author.

Unger, H. (1986, April 17). The people trauma of major mergers. *Journal of Industrial Management* (Canada), *10*, p. 17.

University of Groningen. (1986). *Ongewensta intimiteiten op het werk*. Groningen, Netherlands: Author.

U.S. Merit Systems Protection Board. (1980). *Sexual harassment of federal workers: Is it a problem?* Washington, DC: Government Printing Office.

U.S. Merit Systems Protection Board. (1988). *Sexual harassment of federal workers: An update*. Washington, DC: Government Printing Office.

Wallas, G. (1926). The art of thought. In P. E. Vernon (Ed.), *Creativity*. Hammondsworth, UK: Penguin.

Walsh, J. P. (1988). Top management turnover following mergers and acquisitions. *Strategic Management Journal, 9*, 173-183.

Warr, P. B. (1982). A national study of non-financial employment commitment. *Journal of Occupational Psychology, 51*(2), 183-196.

Warr, P. B. (1987). *Work, unemployment and mental health*. Oxford, UK: Oxford University Press.

Watts, M., & Cooper, C. L. (1992). *Relax: Dealing with stress*. London: BBC Books.

AUTHOR INDEX

Acheson, D., 69
Adair, J., 121, 122
Akersted, T., 104
Albrecht, K., 7, 8
Alpert, D., 149
Altendorf, D. M., 43
Andre, M., 49
Aronson, E., 127
Aronsson, G., 48
Arsenault, A., 49

Barron, A., 105
Bart, P. B., 86
Basowitz, H., 5
Beals, C., 114
Berne, E., 96
Beutell, N. J., 149
Bradley, G., 48

Bransford, J., 137
Breslow, L., 15, 120
Buck, V., 18
Buell, P., 15, 120
Burke, T., 91
Burney, F., 103
Burt, A., 143, 160

Campbell-Moore, B., 150
Cannon, W., 4
Caplan, R. D., 16, 75
Carroll, L., 95
Carruthers, M. E., 10, 11
Cartwright, S., 22, 33, 35, 36, 37, 41,
        44, 51, 55, 60, 105
Cascio, W. F., 55
Catterton, N., 126
Chalykoff, J., 49

Cobb, S., 14, 75

Coch, L., 20

Cohen, L. R., 83

Colatosi, C., 83, 87

Cooper, C. L., 2, 5, 6, 13, 14, 16, 20, 21,
  22, 33, 35, 36, 37, 44, 65, 68, 71,
  75, 76, 77, 105, 129, 146, 148,
  149, 151, 154, 156, 157

Cooper, R. D., 2, 13, 146

Cox, C., 68, 71, 96, 97, 100, 129

Cox, M., 96, 97, 100

Cox, T., 5

Crull, P., 84

Culbertson, A., 149

Cummings, T., 5, 6

Cwitco, G., 49

Dale, B., 13

Di Tecco, D., 49

du Rivage, V., 49

Eaker, L. H., 2, 13, 146

Earnshaw, J., 13

Eggert, M., 56

French, J. R. P., 16, 20, 75

Froggatt, H., 106

Gilbert, L. A., 150

Greenhaus, J. H., 149

Grinker, R. R., 5

Gutek, B. A., 84

Hall, F. S., 146, 147

Hall, T., 146, 147

Handy, C., 143, 145, 146

Harris, T. A., 123, 124

Harrison, R., 27

Heller, J., 67, 75

Herriot, P., 51

Hinkle, L. E., 3, 4

Holmes, T., 41, 51, 55, 60

Holmes, T. H., 32

Holohan, C. K., 150

Hopson, B., 61, 114, 115

Hurrell, J. J., Jr., 22

Hurrell, S., 20

Ivancevich, J. M., 13, 17, 32, 155

Jensen, I. W., 84

Joeman, L. M., 81, 82,

Johannson, G., 48

Johnson, M., 137

Karasek, R., 2

Karchin, S. J., 5

Karg, E., 83, 87

Keita, G. P., 22

Kochan, T. A., 49

Kroes, W., 20

Lazarus, R. S., 5

Levinson, H., 19

Lewis, S., 21, 148, 149, 156, 157

Licata, B. J., 90

Liff, S., 48

Liukkonen, P., 22

Lunde-Jensen, P., 2

Maddock, S., 91

Makin, P., 68, 129

Manning, L., 150

Margolis, B., 20

Marshall, J., 154

Matteson, M. T., 13, 17, 155

McCann, T., 92

McClelland, D. C., 69

McCormack, M., 131
McNeil, E. B., 127
Medea, A., 86
Melhuish, A., 6, 8
Mirvis, P. H., 32
Morrison, E. W., 50
Murphy, L. R., 22

Nelson, S., 36
Nelson-Bolles, R., 61
Nielson, R., 93, 94
Nussbaum, K., 49

Oldham, G. R., 117
Osler, W., 4

Payne, R., 75
Persky, H., 5
Phillips, C. M., 81, 82
Pincherle, A., 17
Pinneau, S. R., 75
Pitturro, M. C., 49
Popovich, P. M., 90
Power, F. R., 32

Quick, J. C., 17, 77
Quick, J. D., 17, 77
Quinn, R., 20

Rahe, R. H., 32
Richards, E. P., 13
Robinson, S. L., 50
Rose, A., 91
Rose, R. H., 14
Rousseau, D. M., 50
Rubenstein, M., 89

Rubin, Z., 127
Russek, H. I., 15

Sadri, G., 22
Sauter, J. T., 20
Sauter, S. L., 22
Scally, M., 61, 114, 115
Schweiger, D. M., 32
Searby, F., 36
Selye, H., 4, 18, 67
Shankley, B., 134
Smith, M. J., 14
Sparrow, P. R., 49
Spindler, S. G., 50
Stamp, P., 106
Stockdale, J. E., 81, 82
Studner, P., 62
Super, D., 64

Theorell, T., 2
Thompson, K., 86
Torrington, D., 65
Townend, A., 114, 115

Unger, H., 37

Van Harrison, R., 75

Wallas, G., 126
Walsh, J. P., 37
Warr, P. B., 53, 55
Watts, M., 76, 77, 151

Zohman, B. L., 15

SUBJECT INDEX

Absenteeism, 2, 13
Acceptance, mergers and, 33
Accidents, 2
    car, 104-105
    intoxicated workers and, 10
Accommodator pattern, dual-career
    families and, 147
Accountability, "new" employment
    contract and, 51
Achievement(s):
    curriculum vitae and, 61
    marriage needs and, 144-145
    technology and, 48
    wheeler-dealers and, 72
Achievement cultures, 29-30
Acquisitions, 31-46
Acrobats, dual-career families and,
    147-148
Activity, job loss and, 53, 54
Adaptation to stress, 4

Adjustment process, 5
Adrenal glands, 7
Adrenaline secretions, 4, 7
Adult ego state, 97
Adversaries, dual-career families and,
    147
Advice, ability to seek, 127
Age, curriculum vitae and, 61
Aging, coping with, 64
Aims, lack of clarity about, 113-114
Air travel, 107-108
Alarm reaction, 4
Alcohol misuse, 10, 65
Allies, dual-career families and, 147
Anal retentive type, meetings and,
    129-130
Anger:
    job loss and, 58
    mergers and acquisitions and, 32,
    37

Angina pectoris, 4
Answering machines, 116
Anxiety, monitoring practices and, 49
Appearance, avoiding sexual
    harassment and, 85
Appraisal, 20
Arteries, reduced elasticity of, 8-10
Assembly line, 14
Assertiveness:
    dealing with sexual harassment
        and, 87, 89, 90
    mushrooms and, 114
    telephone use and, 116
    work overload and, 124-125
Assessments, mergers and
    acquisitions and, 43
Attachment, employment contract
    and, 50
Attention, need to attract, 131
Attitudes:
    "new" employment contract and,
        51
    responding to threatened
        colleagues, 77
Autocrats, 70-72
Automation, 47-48
Autonomic nervous system, 7
Autonomy:
    lack of, 3
    task cultures and, 30
Avoidance, of sexual harassment,
    84-86

Behavior:
    avoiding sexual harassment and,
        85
    organizational culture and, 26
    sexually harassing, 83
    unethical, 91-95
Benefits, unethical behavior and, 92
Bereavement model, job loss and, 56
Biological mechanisms of stress, 6-8
Blood pressure, 7-8
Blood supply, 7

Blood vessels, resistance of, 8
Blue-collar workers, working hours
    and, 120
Boredom, 14
Bosses:
    managing, 68-75
    mergers and acquisitions and, 34
    relationships with, 18
    sexual harassment by, 87-88
    types of, 68-75
Brain, blood supply to, 7
Brainstorming, 133
Britain, see United Kingdom
Budgets, 119
Bureaucracies, 28
Bureaucrats, 69-70
Business ethics, 91-95

Can't do types, 130
Car, travel in, 104-107
Cardiac output, 8
Career(s):
    age-related stages, 64
    changing nature of, 50-51
    dual, 21-22, 143, 146-160
    early choices, 60
    mergers and acquisitions and, 34
    sexual harassment and, 85
    successful change, 41-42
Career advancement, 19
    computers and, 48
    performance measurement and, 50
Career-break schemes, working
    parents and, 158-159
Career consultants, 60
Career development, 19-20
    changing nature of work and, 51
Career structures, adjusting to new,
    47-51
Chairperson, meetings and, 129, 133
Change:
    fundamentals of, 2
    job loss and, 53-64
    middle age and, 66

role cultures and, 29
technological, 47-48
See also Organizational change
Charismatic leader, 27
Child ego state, 97
Christian teaching, self-sacrifice and, 123
Client relationships, 78-80
Climate, sexual harassment and, 88
Clothing, avoiding sexual harassment and, 85
Cohesiveness, organizational culture and, 26
Colleagues:
    relationships with, 19, 75-78
    "shopping," 131-132
Commitment:
    employment contract and, 50
    "new" employment contract and, 51
    open managers and, 74, 75
Communication, 95-101
    dual-career families and, 150
    of instructions, 119
    mergers and acquisitions and, 35, 39, 45-46
    mushrooms and, 114
    poor delegators and, 111
    presentations and, 134
    telephone and, 116
    transactional analysis and, 96-101
Communities:
    family responsibility and, 160
    person/support cultures and, 30
Compensation claims, 2, 13
Competition:
    colleagues and, 76-78
    economic, 2, 119
    international, 2
    role cultures and, 29
Compliance, social conditioning and, 123
Computer technology, 47, 48
Concentrated work, 115

Confrontation, sexual harassment and, 87, 90
Conscientious objection, unethical behavior and, 94
Consensus:
    meetings and, 130, 132
    unethical behavior and, 94-95
Consolidation, middle age and, 65
Contract employees, 50
Control:
    changed career expectations and, 51
    constructive self-talks and, 77
    participation in decision making and, 20
Control, lack of, 2, 3
    mergers and acquisitions and, 33-34
    performance measurement and, 49
    time pressures and, 109-110
Cooperatives, person/support cultures and, 30
Cooper-Cummings framework, 7
Coping strategies, 5
Coronary arteries, fatty deposition in, 10
Coronary heart disease, *see* Heart disease
Corticosteroid hormones, 7
Costs of stress, 2, 10-13
Counseling:
    dual-career families and, 151
    job loss and, 59
    mergers and acquisitions and, 36
    sexual harassment and, 89
Counterdependents, 130-131
Courting cues, 83
Creative cycle, 126
Creativity, task cultures and, 30
Crossed transaction, 99
Cultural messages, self-sacrifice and, 123
Cumulative stress disorder, 13, 24
Curriculum vitae, 57-58, 61-62
Customer relationships, 78-80

Customer service:
  cost-efficient, 49
  monitoring practices and, 49
  organizational culture and, 26
  power cultures and, 27
  role cultures and, 29
  task cultures and, 30

Daily hassles at work, 23
Danger, awareness of in mergers and
    acquisitions, 45
Deadlines, unrealistic, 112
Death, unemployed men and, 55
Decision making:
  groups and, 93
  meetings and, 132
  participation in, 20
  power cultures and, 27
Decline stage, career and, 64
Defense mechanisms, 6-8
Delegation, 18, 111-112, 122, 124
Demotion, fear of, 19
Denial stage, mergers and, 32
Departments:
  role cultures and, 29
  task cultures and, 30
Dependency:
  poor delegators creating, 119
  unemployment and, 53
Depression:
  job loss and, 58
  mergers and, 32
De-stress, 3
Diabetes, shift work and, 14
Difficult people, 68-80
Disability, 13
Disbelief stage, mergers and, 32
Discrimination, sexual harassment
    and, 82
Dismissal, unethical behavior and,
    93-94
Disorganized persons, 112-113
Diversification, middle age and, 66
Divisions of labor:

gender, 48
role cultures and, 28
Divorcees, likelihood of sexual
    harassment and, 86
Divorce rates, 10
Dominance, marriage and, 144-145
Downsizing, 55, 119
Droppers by, interruptions from, 117,
    118
Dual-career family, 21-22, 143, 146-160

Economic competition, 119
Economic pressures, 2
Efficiency:
  improving personal, 124-127
  performance measurement and, 49
Egalitarianism, 30
Ego states, transactional analysis and:
  Adult ego state, 96-101
  Child ego state, 96-101
  Parent ego state, 96-101
Emotion(s):
  Child ego state and, 97
  meetings and, 129
  steady state, 5
Emotional coping, job search and,
    63-64
Employability, 51
Employee(s), surveillance of, 49
Employee participation:
  decision making and, 20, 50, 74
  mergers and acquisitions and, 36
Employment agencies, 62
Employment contracts, short-term, 50
Employment Protection
    (Consolidation) Act (U.K.), 89
Empowerment, 50, 160
Energy levels, 113
Enterprise Culture, 1
Environment:
  fitting into, 26
  interdependence with, 123
  misfit with, 5
  physical arrangement of, 125

Environmental causes of stress, 4-5
Environmental sexual harassment, 80
Ergonomics, car travel and, 106
Establishment stage, career and, 64
Ethnic minorities, likelihood of sexual
 harassment and, 86
Europe, stress costs and, 11-13
European Community, Social Charter,
 15
European Union, 2
Evaluation, 20
Everyday stressful events, 102-142
Exercise, self-image and, 63
Exhaustion stage, 4
Expectations:
 employment contract and, 50-51
 role, 16-17
Expectations of employees,
 organizational culture and, 26
Expense account fraud, 95
Expertise, task cultures and, 30
Expert power, 71
Exploration stage, career and, 64
External report, of sexual harassment,
 88-89
Eye strain, 14

Family:
 changing nature of, 143-146
 dual-career, 21-22, 143, 146-160
 mergers and acquisitions and, 38
 relocations and, 21-22, 153-157
 working hours and, 120
 work stresses and, 21-22
Family goals, 41
Fantasy effect, job loss and, 59
Fatigue:
 travel and, 104
 work space and, 125
Fats, release of, 7, 10
Fear-the-worst syndrome, mergers
 and acquisitions and, 37-38
Feet, cold, 8
Females, *see* Women

Fight-or-flight reaction, 4, 6, 10
Financial consequences, of job loss,
 54, 55, 57
Flexibility, "new" employment
 contract and, 51
Formal complaints, sexual
 harassment and, 83, 85, 87-89
Fragmentation, managers and, 117
Freelancing, 51
Future:
 focusing on, 41
 mergers and acquisitions and, 35,
 45

Gender-based expectations, 86
Gender division of labor, computers
 and, 48
Gender stereotypes, 123, 144, 148
Global economy, 2
Glucose release, 7
Goals:
 individual, 53
 nonwork-related, 41
Going along, unethical behavior and,
 93-94
Great Britain, *see* United Kingdom
Groups:
 autocrats and, 71-72
 decisions by, 93
 managing meetings of, 128-133
 relationships among members of,
 18, 67

Hands, cold, 8
Harm, unethical behavior and, 92
Health:
 people at work affecting, 67
 relationships with colleagues and,
 75
 sexual harassment and, 84
 See also Illness
Health care costs, 2, 11
Health insurance, 2, 11

Heart disease, 2, 4, 10, 11
    long hours and, 15, 120
    working mothers and,
        120-121
Heart rate, 7
Hidden agendas, meetings and, 129
High blood pressure,
    see Hypertension
Holidays, 125-126
Home:
    working at, 47-48
    workload at, 126
    work pressures and, 21-22,
        143-160
Hormones, 6, 7
Hostility, sexual harassment
    and, 80
Hours of work, *see* Working hours
Human factors, car accidents and,
    104-105
Hypertension, 8-10, 14
Hypothalamus, 7

Identity, job loss and, 53-54
Illness:
    unemployed men and, 55
    See also specific illnesses
Illumination stage, creative cycle and,
    126
Inadequacies, admitting, 127-128
Income, job loss and, 53, 54
Incubation stage, creative cycle and,
    126
Inefficiency, 121
Interactions:
    organizational culture and, 26
    transactional analysis and, 96-101
    See also Communication
Internal report, of sexual harassment,
    87-88
International competition, 2
Interpersonal contact, work function
    of, 53, 63

Interruptions, managing, 115-119

Japan, new technology causing stress
    in, 16
Jet lag, 108
Job(s):
    deskilling, 47
    working at two, 15
Job club, 57
Job factors, stress and, 14-16
Job insecurity, 21
Job interviews, 62-63
Job loss:
    coping with, 53-64
    mergers and acquisitions activity,
        31, 34
    sense of rejection and, 52
    technological change and, 47
Job performance, *see* Performance
Job satisfaction:
    freelancing and, 51
    mergers and acquisitions and, 44
    monitoring practices and, 49
    participation in decision making
        and, 20
    relationships with colleagues and,
        75
Job search campaign, preparing
    systematic, 59-63
Job security, 19-20
    mergers and acquisitions and, 31
    outsourcing and, 50
    technological change and, 47
Joint ventures, 2, 31, 33

Labor laws, 3
Labor-saving devices, 126
Larks, 113
Laws:
    labor, 3
    sexual harassment and, 82
    worker compensation, 13

Legal action, 13
    sexual harassment and, 88-89
    unethical behavior and, 94
Life, maintaining as normal during
    merger process, 45-46
Life goals, 41
Life positions, fundamental, 123-125
Lighting, 14
Local-authority careers service, 61
Loneliness, 14
Loss:
    mergers and acquisitions activity
      and, 31, 32-33
    See also Job loss
Lung cancer, unemployed men and,
    55
Lung function, 7

Maintenance stage, career and, 64
Males, *see* Men
Management:
    mergers and acquisitions and, 36
    power cultures and, 27
Management style:
    autocrats and, 71
    bureaucrats and, 70
    open managers and, 75
    organizational culture and, 26
    reluctant managers and, 74
    wheeler-dealers and, 72
Manager(s):
    family versus job transfers and,
      21-22
    fragmentation and, 117
    meeting time and, 128
    mergers and, 46
    open, 74-75
    relocations and, 153
    reluctant, 73-74
    stepping down, 66
    technical backgrounds, 18-19, 73
    time logs and, 121
    types of, 68-75

    working hours and, 120
Managerial jobs:
    searching for, 62
    temporary, 63-64
    verbal communication skills and,
      134
Managing the boss, 68-75
Manual workers, working hours and,
    120
Marriage:
    patterns, 143-146
    problems in, 120, 150-152
    working hours and, 120
Maternal role, traditional attitudes
    and, 150
Maternity leave, 158
Mechanical model of stress, 5
Medical expenses, 2, 11
Meetings, managing, 128-133
Memory aids, presentations
    and, 138
    marriage and, 144-146
Men:
    middle age and, 65
    sexual harassment by, 80-90
    sexual harassment of, 81
    speaking and, 138
    unemployment effects on, 55
    work ethic, 148
Mental monologues:
    mergers and acquisitions and,
      40-45
    responding to threatened
      colleagues, 77
Mergers and acquisitions, 2,
    31-46
Middle age, coping with,
    64-66
Midlife crisis, 64-65
Minutes, meeting, 133
Money, as motivator, 53
Monitoring systems, performance
    and, 49
Mood, senses affecting, 14

Moral codes of behavior, 91
Motivation:
    money as, 53
    "new" employment contract
        and, 51
Muscles, blood supply to, 7
Mushrooms, 113-115
Mutual exchange, employment
    contract and, 50

Negative mental monologues:
    mergers and acquisitions and,
        40-45
    responding to threatened
        colleagues, 77
Negotiation, unethical behavior and,
    94-95
Negotiation mode, mergers and
    acquisitions and, 45
Networking, job search and, 62
Night owls, 113
No, inability to say, 102, 111, 122
Noise, 14
Norms, organizational culture and, 26
North American Free Trade
    Association, 2

Objectives, lack of clarity about, 113-
    114
Obsolescence, fear of, 19
Occupational health hazard, sexual
    harassment as, 84
Occupational psychologists, 60
Office politics, 19
Older workers, job loss and, 54, 55-56
Open manager, 74-75
Open University, 61
Opportunity, job loss as, 57, 60
Oral presentations, 134
Organization(s):
    helping working parents, 157-160
    role in, 16-18
Organizational change, 2, 25-51

acquisitions and, 31-46
    coping with consequences of, 52-66
    mergers and, 31-46
    nature of work and careers, 50-51
    organizational culture and, 25-31
    power cultures and, 28
Organizational climate, 20
Organizational culture, 25-31
    mergers and acquisitions and, 43
    unethical behavior and, 91
Organizational performance,
    unethical behavior and, 91
Organizational stock taking, mergers
    and acquisitions and, 43
Organizational structure, 20
    delayered, 51, 119
    organizational culture and, 26
Outplacement facilities, 59, 60
Outsourcing, 50
Overload, work, 16

Pain, stress and, 2
Paper shuffling, 110
Parasympathetic nerves, 8
Parent(s), organizations helping,
    157-160
Parent ego state, 96-97
Participative management practices,
    50, 74
Part-time work, 63
Patriarchal power cultures, 28
Pay:
    as motivator, 53
    "new" employment contract and,
        51
    performance-related, 49
People at work:
    difficult, 68-80
    relationships with, 18-19, 67-101
People issues, mergers and
    acquisitions and, 36-37
Performance, 20
    jet lag and, 108
    sexual harassment and, 84

travel and, 104
unethical behavior and, 91
Performance measurement, 49-50
Personal growth and development,
    organizational culture
    and, 30
Personality:
    abrasive, hard-driving, 19
    Type A, 72
    Type B, 74
Personality needs:
    autocrats and, 70-71
    bureaucrats and, 69
    open managers and, 74-75
    reluctant managers and, 73-74
    wheeler-dealers and, 72
Personal power, 72
Personal responsibility, unethical
    behavior and, 92
Personal role definition, 149
Personal stock taking:
    curriculum vitae and, 58
    mergers and acquisitions and,
    41-43
Person/support cultures, 30-31
Physical conduct, sexual harassment
    and, 84
Physical consequences:
    long hours and, 15, 120
    shift work and, 14
Physical factors:
    car travel and, 106
    rail and air travel and, 108
Physical health, *see* Health
Physical reactions:
    to sexual harassment, 86-87
    to stress, 4, 6-8
Planning:
    changed career expectations and,
    51
    presentations and, 135-137
    telephone use, 116
    time management and, 112-113
Policies and procedures, sexual
    harassment and, 88

Position power, 70
Positive mental monologue,
    responding to threatened
    colleagues and, 77
Power:
    autocrats and, 70, 71
    breadwinner and, 148
    bureaucrats and, 70
    mergers and acquisitions and, 35
    open managers and, 74
    reluctant managers and, 73-74
    sexual harassment and, 83, 86, 89
    wheeler-dealers and, 72
Power cultures, 27-28
Preparation stage, creative cycle
    and, 126
Presentations, 134-142
Press, talking to, 141-142
Privacy, invasion of, 49
Problems, self-created, 102
Problem solving, admitting
    inadequacies and, 127
Procrastination, 110
Productivity, 2, 13, 121
    monitoring practices and, 49
    people at work affecting, 67
    relationships with colleagues
    and, 75
    telephone use and, 116
    working hours and, 120
Professional partnerships,
    person/support cultures and,
    30
Profit maximization, business ethics
    and, 91
Promotion, *see* Career advancement
Psychiatric injury, claims for, 13
Psychological consequences:
    of job loss, 54, 55, 56-59
    sexual harassment and, 84, 89
    unethical behavior and, 93-94
Psychological culture of organization,
    25-31
Punishment, power cultures and, 28
Purpose:

job loss and, 53, 54, 63
lack of clarity about, 113-114

Qualitative overload, 16, 120
Quantitative overload, 16, 120
Questions, presentations and, 140-141
Quid pro quo sexual harassment, 80
Quiet hours, 116, 117-118

Rail travel, 107-108
Rape crisis centers, 89
Reactive role behavior, 149
Red herring types, 130
Reemployment, chances of gaining,
     55-56
Regulations, 3
     bureaucrats and, 69, 70
     Parent ego state and, 96
Rejection, sense of, 52
Relationships at work, 18-19, 67-101
     with bosses, 18, 68-75
     client, 78-80
     with colleagues, 19, 75-78
     customer, 78-80
     overdependent, 119
     poor delegators and, 111
     steady state, 5
     with subordinates, 18-19
     transactional analysis and, 96-101
Relaxation, 8
     car travel and, 106-107
     creativity and, 126-127
     rail and air travel and, 108
Relocations, family and, 21-22, 153-157
Reluctant manager, 73-74
Resignations:
     mergers and acquisitions and, 37
     sexual harassment and, 84-85
Resistance to stress, 4
Resource power, 70
Responsibility, 17-18
Retaliation, sexual harassment and, 87
Rewards:

employment contract and, 50, 51
performance measurement and, 50
power cultures and, 28
Role(s), 16-17
     dual-career families, 147-150
     gender, 123
     meetings and, 129-132
     sexual harassment and, 86, 90
Role ambiguity, 17
Role conflict, 17
Role cultures, 28-29
Role duplicity, mergers and
     acquisitions and, 35
Role expansion, 149
Role negotiation techniques, sexual
     harassment and, 90
Rules, 3
     bureaucrats and, 69-70
     Parent ego state and, 96
     reluctant managers and, 73
Rumors, mergers and acquisitions
     and, 45-46

Sabbaticals, working parents and, 159
Sanctions:
     autocrats and, 71
     bureaucrats and, 70
     open managers and, 75
     reluctant managers and, 74
     wheeler-dealers and, 72
Sanity breaks, 125
Scientific backgrounds, managers
     with, 18
Self-created problems, 102
Self-employment, 51
Self-esteem:
     job loss and, 58
     unemployment and, 54
Self-help group, 57
Self-help manuals and courses, job
     seekers and, 61
Self-image:
     exercise and, 63
     sexual harassment and, 85

Self-initiative, changed career
    expectations and, 51
Self-sacrifice, 123
Self-talk:
    mergers and acquisitions and,
        40-45
    responding to threatened
        colleagues, 77
Senses, bombardment of, 14
Sex Discrimination Act of 1975 (U.K.),
    88-89
Sexual attraction, in workplace, 83
Sexual harassment, 80-90
    categories of, 84
    impact of, 83-85
    stopping, 85-89
    types of, 80
Shift work, 14
Single-income families,
    unemployment and, 55
Single parents, likelihood of sexual
    harassment and, 86
Single people, unemployment
    and, 55
Skills:
    curriculum vitae and, 58
    deskilling jobs and, 47
    unemployment and, 54, 63
Sleep:
    shift work and, 14
    travel and, 104, 108
Smells, 14
Smoking, women and, 120
Social class, cultural messages
    reinforcing, 123
Social isolation:
    mergers and, 46
    working at home and, 48
Socialization:
    gender roles and, 148
    overwork and, 122-123
Social stigma, unemployment and, 54
Social support, 19
    colleagues and, 75
    mergers and acquisitions and, 38

Society, family role expectations and,
    148
Stability, range of, 5
State employment offices, 61
Status:
    likelihood of sexual harassment
        and, 86
    role cultures and, 29
    work defining, 53
Steady state, 5
Stepping down, middle age and, 66
Strain, 3-4, 5
Stress:
    assessing, 10-11
    biological mechanisms of, 6-8
    costs of, 2, 10-13
    defining, 3-6
    growing epidemic of, 1-24
    pain and, 2
    stages, 4
    See also Workplace stress
Stressful events, everyday, 102-142
Stress management courses, mergers
        and acquisitions and, 36
Stress reaction, 5
Stroke, 10
Structure, *see* Organizational structure
Structure role definition, 148-149
Subordinates, relationships with,
    18-19
Suggestions, appropriating, 131
Suicide, 10, 55
Superwoman image, 120
Support, sexual harassment and, 89
Sympathetic nervous system, 7, 8

Taking on too much, 122-125
Talker, constant, 129
Target setting, 49-50, 119
Task/achievement cultures, 29-30
Team culture, 30
Technical backgrounds, managers
        with, 18-19, 73
Technology:

change and, 47-48
stress caused by, 16
Telephone:
    car, 106
    controlling use of, 113
    interruptions from, 116
Temporal structure, job providing, 53,
    54
Temporary workers, 63
    managerial, 63-64
Thoughts, steady state, 5
Threat(s):
    mergers and acquisitions and, 45
    stress reaction and, 5-6
Threatened colleagues, 76-78
Time log, 121-122
Time management, 108-115, 121
    car accidents and, 105
    meetings and, 132
Time of day, energy level and, 113
Time-out periods, marriages and, 151,
    152-153
Time-saving devices, 126
To do list, 110, 113
Total quality management, 78
Training:
    assertiveness, 90, 114
    changing nature of work and, 51
    computer users, 48
    employment contract and, 50
    job seekers and, 60, 61
Tranquillity, 8
Transactional analysis, 96-101
Transfers:
    family and, 21-22, 153-157
    mergers and acquisitions and, 34
    middle age and, 65
    sexual harassment and, 84
Travel, stress caused by, 16, 103-108
Trust:
    delegation and, 111
    performance measurement and, 49
    relationships with colleagues
        and, 75

Turnover, 13
    mergers and acquisitions and, 37
Type A personality, 72
Type B personality, 74

Ulcers, shift work and, 14
Ulterior transactions, 100
Uncertainty:
    mergers and acquisitions and, 33,
        35
    unemployment and, 54
Unemployment, 53-64
    emotional cycle associated with,
        56-59
Unemployment benefits, 57
Unethical behavior, 91-95
Union, reporting sexual harassment
    to, 87, 88
United Kingdom:
    costs of stress, 2, 10
    female labor force, 146
    litigation in, 13
    mergers and acquisitions activity,
        31
    new technology causing stress in,
        16
    sexual harassment in, 81-82
    sexual harassment reports and,
        88-89
    working women in, 21
United States:
    costs of stress, 2
    downsizing in, 55
    sexual harassment in, 81
    stress-related illnesses in, 11
    traditional families and, 146
    working women in, 21
Unknown, presentations and, 135

Values:
    organizational culture and, 26
    Parent ego state and, 97

unethical behavior and, 92, 93
Verbal conduct, sexual harassment
   and, 84
Verification stage, creative cycle and,
   126
Visiting hours, 118
Visual aids, presentations and, 138-139
Visual conduct, sexual harassment
   and, 84
Voluntary work, 63
V-time (voluntary reduced time),
   157-158

West Germany, sexual harassment
   and, 82
Wheeler-dealer boss, 72-73
Whistle blowing, unethical behavior
   and, 94
White-collar workers:
   unemployment and, 55
   working hours and, 49, 120
Widows, likelihood of sexual
   harassment and, 86
Women, 146
   career breaks and, 158
   car safety and, 105-106
   computer use and, 48
   conditioning to be acquiescent, 123
   full-time careers, 21-22
   heart disease and, 120-121
   leaving work to become mothers,
      53-54
   marriage and, 144-146
   meeting role and, 131
   organizations helping working,
      157-160
   sexual harassment of, 80-90
   smoking by, 120
   speaking and, 138
   traditional attitudes, 150
   unemployment effects on, 55
   working hours and, 120-121
   workload at home, 126

Work:
   changing nature of, 50-51
   daily hassles at, 23
   functions for individual, 53
   home interface, 143-160
   meaning derived from, 52
   relationships at, 18-19, 67-101
   sexual attraction at, 83
Work ethic, 54, 148
Worker compensation, 2, 13
Working arrangements, adjusting to
   new, 47-51
Working conditions, 14
   technology and, 48
Working hours, 15, 120
   parents and, 157-158
   performance measurement
      and, 49
Working parents, organizations
   helping, 157-160
Workload, 2, 119-128
Work overload, 16, 120
Workplace design, 14
Workplace stresses, 13-22
   acquisitions, 31-46
   career development, 19-20
   changing nature of work and
      careers, 50-51
   communication within work
      environment and, 95-101
   difficult people and, 68-80
   everyday events and, 102-142
   factors intrinsic to job, 14-16
   family and, 21-22
   home-work interface and,
      143-160
   ingredients of, 2-3
   interruptions, 115-119
   job loss and, 53-64
   meetings and, 128-133
   mergers, 31-46
   new working arrangements,
      47-51
   organizational change and, 52-66

organizational cultures and
   change, 25-51
organizational structure and
   climate, 20
performance measurement and,
   49-50
person's role in organization and,
   16-18
presentations and, 134-142
relationships at work, 18-19,
   67-101
relocations and, 21-22, 153-158

sexual harassment, 80-90
time management and, 108-115
travel and, 103-108
unethical behavior and, 91-95
working hours and, 15, 120
workload and, 2, 119-128
Workplace stresses, 13-22
Work space, physical arrangement of,
   125
Worrying, mergers and acquisitions
   and, 45
Worthlessness, feelings of, 124

ABOUT THE
AUTHORS

Susan Cartwright, PhD, is Senior Research Fellow in the Centre for Business Psychology of the Manchester School of Management, University of Manchester Institute of Science and Technology (UMIST). She has published widely in the area of organizational stress, mergers and acquisitions, and organizational culture and change. She is a Chartered Occupational Psychologist, Associate Fellow of the British Psychological Society, and coauthor of the book *No Hassle! Taking the Stress out of Work* (1994).

Cary L. Cooper is currently Professor of Organizational Psychology at the Manchester School of Management, University of Manchester Institute of Science and Technology (UMIST). He is the author of more than 70 books (on occupational stress, women at work, and industrial and organizational psychology), has written more than 250 scholarly articles for academic journals, and is a frequent contributor to national newspapers, TV, and radio. He is currently Editor-in-Chief of the *Journal of Organizational Behavior*, coeditor of the medical journal *Stress Medicine*, and Fellow of the British Psychological Society and the Royal Society of Arts.